VENTRILOQUISM
Magic with Your Voice

GEORGE SCHINDLER

ILLUSTRATED BY
ED TRICOMI

DOVER PUBLICATIONS, INC.
MINEOLA, NEW YORK

Bibliographical Note

This Dover edition, first published in 2011, is an unabridged republication of the work originally published by David McKay Co., New York, in 1979.

Library of Congress Cataloging-in-Publication Data

Schindler, George.
   Ventriloquism : magic with your voice / George Schindler ; illustrated by Ed Tricomi.—Dover ed.
      p. cm.
   Originally published: New York : D. McKay Co., c1979.
   Includes bibliographical references.
   ISBN-13: 978-0-486-47760-2
   ISBN-10: 0-486-47760-6
      1. Ventriloquism. I. Tricomi, Ed, ill. II. Title.

GV1557.S33 2011
793.8'9—dc22

2010028791

Manufactured in the United States by Courier Corporation
47760601
www.doverpublications.com

To Howard Olson and to the memory
of Paul Stadelman, who put the two
of us together

CONTENTS

FOREWORD

I was eleven years old when my cousin Julius received a gift of a large Charlie McCarthy ventriloquist doll. It was magnificent—dressed in a smart black tuxedo and wearing a top hat and a small monocle in one eye. You operated his mouth by pulling a string that came from a small hole in the back of his neck. Julius and I took turns pretending we were Edgar Bergen and trying to make the little fellow talk. Neither of us was too successful. We looked and sounded nothing like the characters in the Edgar Bergen movies we tried to mimic. Julius gave up first, put the doll aside, and learned to play the trumpet instead. I tried and tried but had no idea how to change my voice or how to stop my lips from moving. I finally gave up and went back to my magic tricks.

A few years later I was fortunate to meet and later assist Abe Hurwitz, who performed magic in the New York City parks as "Peter Pan the Magic Man." "Doc," as we called him, formed a magic club with youngsters like me who were interested. The group was great fun, and thanks to Abe's guidance many of us eventually became professionals. Among the people in our group were Stan Burns, Len Cooper, George Gilbert, Al Goshman, Ken Krenzel, Jack London, Danny O'Bryan, George Sands, and Howie Schwartzman.

Each year Doc would tutor our little group and we would produce a grand magic show at the Central Park mall. It was held on Columbus Day, when lots of people were in the park before or after the parades. I can remember one show in which I performed a trick called the "Arabian Tent Illusion." I put

The author's first public appearance as a ventriloquist with Matilda in 1942.

together a few panels resembling the sides of a tent. When I added the roof and clapped my hands, a small girl would pop out of the empty tent. It was Doc's daughter Shari. She burst onto the center of the stage wearing a colorful satin costume. The music came up full—amplified from a phonograph offstage—and Shari would dance. Shari is still dancing in her Las Vegas nightclub act. Her stage name is Shari Lewis.

In 1942 we needed a ventriloquist act for our magic show. Doc knew that I loved to watch ventriloquists and was fascinated by them. One afternoon he pointed a finger at me and said, "Georgie, you will be our ventriloquist." He gave me about three weeks to learn the art. I couldn't even pronounce the word. Doc presented me with a cute little "vent" figure one of the other fellows had made. It had a movable head and mouth control string on the headstick, just like a professional figure. While I was thrilled with the idea, it wasn't what I had expected. This doll was a little *girl*. Not only did I have to learn how to manipulate the figure, but I had to develop a female voice for my new partner.

"It's easy," counseled Doc. "All you have to do is change your voice when she talks. Don't move your lips. Make believe she's real." And so I became a ventriloquist.

In three weeks I had taught myself the obvious methods of pronouncing words without lip movement. I avoided the difficult sounds by writing them out of my script. In the act I blindfolded my little girl, Matilda. We did a comedy mind-reading satire and performed as "George and Matilda, the Wooden Mentalist."

In this book you will learn everything you should know about the technical aspects of ventriloquism. You will learn that the most important reason for performing as a ventriloquist is to entertain your audience. You will learn how to manipulate your figure or puppet to help you make believe it's real. When you can make others believe that your partner is real, you are a ventriloquist.

1

VENTRILOQUISM

What Is It?

Some of you may remember the merchandise catalogues you read as a child. The ads promised great things for your future and served to make your dreams more colorful and exciting. I was influenced by one ad in particular. It depicted a small boy, wearing a big guilty grin on his face, standing near an older man who was carrying a heavy trunk on his back. The man had a surprised look on his face, for a voice from inside the box was shouting, "Let me out of here!" The caption read, "Throw Your Voice."

For ten cents, almost all of my allowance, I bought the secret device that I could put into my mouth. It was supposed to give me the ability to make my voice come from inside trunks or closets. I was quite disappointed to receive a small swazzle or kind of whistle similar to those used by Punch and Judy workers. By combining it with my own voice, I could vibrate the thin membrane inside the whistle to create funny, high-pitched sounds. But I could not throw my voice.

There is really no such thing as "throwing" your voice. Your own vocal sounds cannot come from across the lake, from inside the dresser drawer, or from a bottle of wine on the table. No gimmicks or whistles or special devices can help you. You can, however, create the *illusion* that your voice is coming from those places. Ventriloquism is the technique of making others think that your voice comes from somewhere other than from you.

The best part is that anyone who can speak can learn the art of ventriloquism. No special vocal apparatus is needed, nor is the ability an inherited talent. Ventriloquists learn the art the same way other people learn to play a musical instrument or learn to sing and dance. First they must learn the rules, and then they must take the time to practice.

Ages ago, people thought that ventriloquists were born with a "double throat" or that they spoke from their stomachs. In fact, the word *ventriloquism,* derived from a French word, comes from the Latin *venter,* which means "stomach" or "belly," and the word *loqui,* which means "I speak." It is true that in producing some sounds, the stomach muscles are involved, but certainly your voice cannot come from anywhere except the vocal cords.

To create the proper illusion, the ventriloquist uses a form of misdirection like the magician. Instead of using sleight of hand, the ventriloquist creates the magic with his voice. He directs the eye of the spectator to the point where he wants the sound to appear. The ventriloquist knows that hearing is the least reliable of the five senses. The eye is always used to verify what the ear has heard. When a sound comes from a place out of your direct line of vision, you often cannot tell exactly where it came from. A fire engine in the distance may sound as if it comes from one direction, when actually it comes from another. You usually turn your head in order to see the fire engine before you accept its actual location.

Try this experiment. Have a friend sit in a chair with his eyes closed. Now tap two coins together directly above his head. Ask him where the sounds came from. He may or may not answer correctly. Strike the coins together again, under his chin. He will tell you the sound came from either the right or the left, or even behind him.

The ventriloquist uses various devices to deceive the spectator's brain even further. To begin with, he uses three categories of ventriloquial voice. For sounds coming from a vent figure or puppet, he uses a *near voice,* or *near ventriloquism.* For the sound of a voice coming out of a suitcase, from behind a door, or from a point not too far away, he uses a muffled *near-distant voice.* And for voices from very far away, he uses, logically, a *distant voice.* You will learn these techniques in this book.

You will note that we never use the term *dummy* to describe any of the characters in this book. The word is not descriptive of the lifelike characters we want to create.

I mentioned *misdirection* a moment ago. This is a magicians' term meaning to distract attention away from the thing the magician is really doing. The ventriloquist creates misdirection in several ways. The most popular, of course, is by using a figure or puppet that has a moving mouth. The eye sees the movement and sends a message to the brain telling it the sound is coming from the doll. Another way in which the ventriloquist misdirects the audience is by making the words he speaks sound different from his normal voice. A third way is by controlling his lips so that he does not give himself away. These three methods are used for *near ventriloquism.*

As we describe more advanced ventriloquism, we will cover the *near distant* and *distant sounds,* and we will add techniques for making the sounds fainter and more muffled as required.

Ventriloquism is a most satisfying talent to develop. A recent survey found that more than 70 percent of the ventriloquists in America entertain in churches and Sunday schools. Fifty percent perform in schools. Only 15 percent are professional television or nightclub performers. Ventriloquism is used by teachers to make the learning process more enjoyable for their students. It is used by evangelists to preach the Gospel. Many doctors have used vent figures to reach brain-damaged children or children with psychological problems. The children will speak more readily to the puppet than to the doctor. Ventriloquism can also be used to help youngsters with stuttering problems. But, of course, the most popular use is for entertainment.

When Did Ventriloquism Begin?

Archaeological evidence found in Egypt gives proof of ventriloquism dating back to 2000 B.C. The use of the art probably goes back to the beginning of intelligible language itself. Mysterious occurrences that gave rise to superstitions can now be explained as possible ventriloquism. For example, many people have believed that spirits could be evoked inside the bodies of certain individuals and that those spirits spoke in a "second voice." The "familiar spirit," as it was called, was never explained. The law, set down by Moses for his people 1,500 years before Christ recognized the belief in familiar spirits and forbade Jews from consulting with them. The spirit's voice was described as "low" and "out of the dust" in a biblical reference by the prophet Isaiah (29:4).

How the Egyptians learned ventriloquial technique has never been made clear, but ventriloquism did exist. It is assumed that unscrupulous priests used it for their own gain. Much like early magic, the secrets of ventriloquism were closely guarded by its users. Throughout history we find that ventriloquists were thought to be possessed of demons, and along with magicians were considered to be in league with the devil.

A temple was built in Delphi in the sixth century B.C. There the Greek oracles spoke the words of Apollo through his priestess Pythia. The woman would chant and utter weird sounds and noises. One of the priests would then interpret these sounds to those seeking the advice of the gods. The words of the oracle helped govern Greece. Sometimes the Greek priests would stand immobile, and strained sounds would come from their stomachs. Their lips would not move as words were formed. They were practicing *gastromancy,* a form of ventriloquism. The early Greeks called the belly-talkers *Eurykliden.* They were named after Euryklides, who produced the sounds of birds and small animals ventriloquially. As suggested earlier, the word *ventriloquism* was derived from the belief that the sounds came from the stomach.

The Bible tells that King Saul consulted the Witch of Endor regarding the outcome of a battle. The witch conjured up the voice of the prophet Samuel, who supposedly spoke from the dead. The voice answered the king's questions. I have no doubt that the Witch of Endor was a very capable ventriloquist.

Ventriloquism has been used for many years in conjunction with religious rites. Often, religious leaders used it to strengthen their powers over ignorant or superstitious followers. Until recently, a few tribes in Africa and in the Pacific Islands listened to their idols speaking. It is believed by some that Eskimos also practiced the art.

Ventriloquism developed as an entertainment form much like

7

its cousin, magic. In 1700 a Spanish count made an "automaton" or mechanical doll that had a movable mouth. King Francis of the Holy Roman Empire was entertained with ventriloquism by Louis Brabant, whose fine talents won him the hand of a beautiful heiress. In 1772 a man named Abbe de la Chapelle published a work describing ventriloquists. Chapelle was a ventriloquist and had admired the talents of such people as M. St. Gille, a grocer who practiced outside of Paris, and Baron von Mengen of Vienna. Von Mengen used seven or eight wooden figures, creating all the voices himself.

Napoleon and Josephine were entertained by Le Sieur Thiemet. At about the same time another ventriloquist, Nicholas Marie Alexander, was doing a one-man show. Nicholas did a play in which he changed costume and acted out various roles. He used his ventriloquism for the offstage replies of his imaginary characters.

Punch and Judy were popular in Italy and then in England, and while not directly related to ventriloquism, puppets led the way for ventriloquists using figures. Many magicians included ventriloquism in their shows, treating it like any other magical illusion. In 1811 Richard Potter advertised that he would "throw his voice into different parts of the room and into the gentlemen's hats, trunks, etc." Potter practiced doing imitations of birds and animal sounds—*polyphony*. In 1840 a Mr. Sutton used a talking automaton that did imitations of the Roman Oracles.

It wasn't until the late 1800s that vent figures became popular. Edwardian and Victorian ventriloquists used figures dressed as soldiers and sailors for their sketches. Fred Neiman, a vent in the 1840s, dressed as a jester and worked with a group of figures on stage. He went from one figure to another, changing his voice and conversing with each one. A man named Fred Russell is credited with the first "knee figure," whom he called Coster Joe. Joe wore a cap and street clothes and, sitting on Russell's knee, gave a most lifelike appearance. This paved the way for more recent vents who played vaudeville.

Three ventriloquists stand out in the history of the art during the early 1900s. One was Arthur Prince. His stage setting was a simple backdrop depicting the deck of a battleship. Prince

VENTRILOQUISM.

Mr.  POTTER,

The VENTRILOQUIST,

Begs leave most respectfully to inform the Ladies
and Gentlemen of · that he intends to give an

Evening's Brush to Sweep away

CARE; Or, A Medley to Please,

At Mr.   Ball-Room,
On   Evening,   instant.

In the course of the Evening will be offered upwards of

100

with Cards, Eggs,

Money, &c.

CURIOUS BUT MYSTERIOUS

Experiments,

(For Particulars, see small Bills.)

A SONG,

by Mr. POTTER.

PART SECOND.

VENTRILOQUISM.

Mr. P. will display his wonderful but laborious powers of Ventriloquism. He throws his voice into many different parts of the room, and into the gentlemen's hats, trunks, &c. Imitates all kinds of Birds and Beasts, so that few or none will be able to distinguish his imitations from the reality. This part of the performance has never failed of exciting the surprise of the learned and well informed, as the conveyance of sounds is allowed to be one of the greatest curiosities of nature.

PART THIRD.

THE WHOLE TO CONCLUDE WITH A RECITATION AND SONG IN CHARACTER OF TIMOTHY NORPOST dressed in a naval officer's uniform and smoked a cigar. His figure, Jim, was dressed as a sailor. Prince sat on a stool next to Jim and the two of them had an amusing dialogue. His assistant would bring out a glass of water, which Prince drank as the figure said, "Going, going, gone!" Arthur Prince popularized ventriloquism; he was a showman and a fine actor who played in theaters everywhere. He died on July 14, 1946.

John W. Cooper was called the "Black Napoleon of Ventriloquism." Cooper was black and learned the art as a hobby in 1895. Starting in 1901 he appeared in minstrel shows, where he earned his reputation. He used unusual figures, such as a walking doll, and was the first to use a talking parrot. In vaudeville, Cooper did a barbershop sketch in which he played the part of the barber. His characters were already seated. Mr. Haskins sat in the barber chair; Miss Auto, a manicurist, sat nearby. A waiting customer sat in another chair, and a bootblack waited for some business. Cooper used foot pedals to operate the various figures. He played in vaudeville as the "Polite Ventriloquist" for many years before retiring. He also taught ventriloquism; his most famous student was Shari Lewis.

Harry Lester began his career in show business as a Hindu magician and fire-eater, using the stage name Kaloofra. His real name was Maryan Czagkowski. He learned ventriloquism and was playing the vaudeville circuits around 1904. Lester developed the technique of using only one chair and a small table in front of the curtain. This is known as working "in one." He also featured the Drinking Trick but was best recognized for his Telephone Routine. The Great Lester, as he was called, spoke with his figure, George Byron, Jr., and the two of them held a conversation on the phone with a second voice, who then was heard calling a third party in a "distant" voice even farther away. The Great Lester was one of vaudeville's highest-paid performers and did command performances for royalty. He appeared all over the United States before settling in California, where he taught other ventriloquists until he died in 1956. One of his most famous students was Edgar Bergen.

Many fine ventriloquists played the vaudeville circuits. Chesterfield was a well-known act in the South and Midwest. He started around 1910 working with two figures, one white and one

10

black. At one point in the act he introduced his small son, Chester LeRoy, who also was a ventriloquist. Chester LeRoy's real name is Howard Olson, and he is now one of the leading makers of fine ventriloquial figures. Olson worked his way from vaudeville to Broadway to radio. In 1950 he had his own television show in Milwaukee.

In the late 1930s Edgar Bergen brought new popularity to the art of ventriloquism.

Edgar Berggren (Bergen) was a Swedish immigrant who earned money with his ventriloquism to help put himself through school at Northwestern University as a premed student. Charlie McCarthy was whittled out of wood in 1922 by Frank Marshall, who worked for the Charlie Mack Company in Chicago. Bergen and Charlie played many local clubs but did not hit it big until an appearance at the Chez Paree in Chicago, where one night Charlie set the act aside and ad-libbed with the customers. Bergen was held over and changed the act by adding more smart quips and ad-libs for Charlie. In 1945 Bergen married Frances Westerman. They had two children, Chris and Candice.

Bergen's work on radio and in movies became so popular that his characters became known all over the world. Many television fans remember his work on the game show "Do You Trust Your Wife?" and on many other shows. Charlie won a wooden "Oscar" that was made with a movable jaw. Although a busy performer all his life, Edgar Bergen still found time to entertain servicemen and women during two wars. A trouper in show business, Bergen worked until the day he died in Las Vegas just before a show, on September 30, 1978. Charlie McCarthy became so much a part of American history that it has been suggested that he be preserved for posterity in a museum of the Smithsonian Institution in Washington, D.C.

The 1960s and 1970s produced many new nightclub and television ventriloquists who all became stars. These were people like Paul Winchell and Jerry Mahoney, Jimmy Nelson and Danny O'Day, and Shari Lewis and her puppet Lambchop. Around the country other vents were playing clubs and theaters. Some of the more popular acts were Jay Marshall and Lefty, Monsieur Brunard, Señor Wences, Roy Douglas, Ricky Layne and Velvel, Howard Olson and Cowboy Eddie, Paul Stadelman

Edgar Bergen with Mortimer Snerd, Charlie McCarthy, and Effie Klinker.

and Windy Higgins, Stan Burns and his Chinese figure Lichi. There were many fine women ventriloquists in the past, such as Kaetie Loisset and Charlotte Bern. Three modern American beauty queens are ventriloquists. Vonda Kay Van Dyke, a former Miss America, Marie McLaughlin, and Sandy Rings. In England, Terri Rogers and her cheeky little boy, Shorty, wow them in the cabarets. The list of well-known names could go on and on, for each year a new face arrives on the show business scene. And, who knows, perhaps you will become one of tomorrow's ventriloquial entertainers.

JOHN W. COOPER

— THE POLITE VENTRILOQUIST —

An early photo of the Great Chesterfield (1911). The figure on the left, now known as Cowboy Eddie, is still being used by Howard Olson.

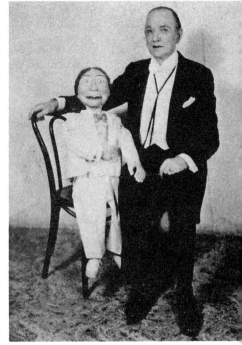

The Great Lester. (Photo courtesy of the Vent Haven Museum)

Doc Dougherty with Willie O'Neal. "Doc Dougherty's Dolls" entertained school children all over the United States from 1945 to 1956. Willie was handcarved by Frank Marshall.

Paul Stadelman and Windy Higgins. Paul started in show business as a magician during the late 1930s. After adopting Windy, which was carved by Charlie Mack, he achieved fame as a vent and later began the first school for ventriloquists in America. Many of his students have become professionals. Although he died some years ago, his books and teaching tapes continue to train young students of the art.

2

BASIC TECHNIQUES

Almost all animals have voices. We know that dogs bark, birds chirp, owls screech, and other animals groan, whistle, howl, or coo. Humans are able to change the many kinds of sounds they make into patterns used for communicating with one another. The human voice arranges the various sounds, juxtaposing vowels and consonants to form words and phrases. That is how we create language. As infants we are taught to form our sounds into meaningful speech by imitating the sounds we hear and by watching the lips of the people who speak to us. When you speak, you really never stop to think about how you are making the sounds; they all seem to come naturally. As a ventriloquist, you will often be required to create and imitate specific sounds. Therefore, a working knowledge of how speech is produced will be very useful to you.

How We Produce Sound

The sound producers in humans are called *vocal cords*. These are two bands of tissue that stretch across the voice box. The technical name of the voice box is the *larynx*. It is located between the back of your tongue and your windpipe. The windpipe is also known as the *trachea*. One cord stretches on each side of the trachea opening. As you breathe, air comes in and out of your lungs, passing through the larynx. Muscles in the larynx stretch and relax the vocal cords. When these muscles are relaxed the air passes through your system without making any

16

noise. The cords are at rest, leaving a small V-shaped opening for the passage of air.

When you speak, the muscles pull on the vocal cords and make the opening even smaller and narrower. The lungs act as bellows and force the air into the windpipe so that the vocal cords are made to vibrate. The tighter the vocal cords are stretched, the higher and more shrill the sound becomes. As the cords are relaxed, the sound becomes lower. When your larynx is irritated or the vocal cords are strained, you may produce no sound at all. People who have *laryngitis* often cannot speak above a whisper.

Here is an experiment you might want to try. You will need a matchbox (the size used for kitchen matches) or any small box. Get three rubber bands of varying sizes. Place the middle-sized rubber band around the open box. The box will act as a sounding board. Snap the rubber band so that it vibrates and listen to the sound it produces. It is almost like the sound of a guitar string. Now use a smaller rubber band. Since it is smaller, it will stretch when you put it around the box, and when you vibrate it, the sound will be higher. The larger rubber band will give you a lower sound. If you used a larger box for the experiment, the sound would change again, for the pitch would be different.

Your vocal cords react the same way the rubber bands in the experiment did (Figure 1). When you speak, you naturally relax or tighten your vocal cords to create the various sounds you need. The size of the larynx controls the pitch of your voice. A young boy speaks with a high voice, but as he reaches the age of puberty and his larynx grows, his voice becomes lower or deeper. For some reason, girls' larynxes rarely change size and their pitch remains stable throughout life.

The quality of your voice is determined by the shape of your nose, throat, and mouth. The color or resonance in the voice is produced by the nasal cavity. Sing "aah" a few times normally. Now try it again, but this time pinch your nose. The sound will change and become more nasal. When you have a cold, your nasal passage or the nasal cavity is clogged, and your voice changes. Sometimes when you are nervous or very tense or excited, your voice will be a bit higher than normal because your muscles are strained. Your lips and teeth also shape the sound of your voice. As you will see later, your tongue is very important for articulation.

17

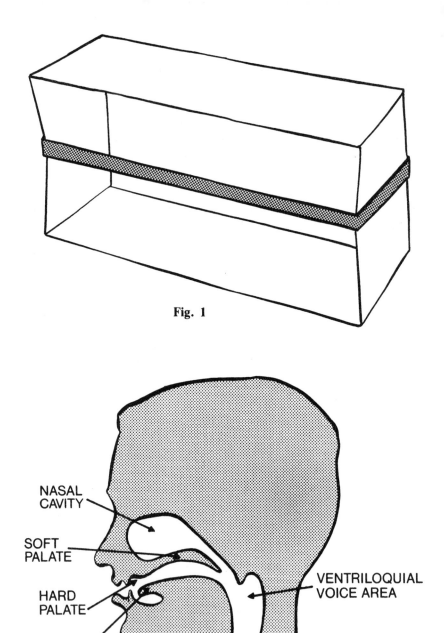

Fig. 1

NASAL CAVITY

SOFT PALATE

HARD PALATE

TONGUE

LARYNX & VOCAL CORDS

VENTRILOQUIAL VOICE AREA

Fig. 2

Let's take a closer look at how we produce sounds, using technical terms for all the important parts of the system. Voice production occurs in the small space inside the larynx between the vocal cords. This space is called the *glottis*. The upper part of the larynx is shaped like a box. It is made of nine sections of soft, flexible material called *cartilage.* In front of the larynx are two wing-shaped plates of cartillage that project from your throat. These sections are called *thyroid cartilage,* but we know it as the *Adam's Apple.* The back wall of the larynx is a rim-shaped form called the *cricoid cartilage.*

As we go further into our studies we will use other terms with which you should be familiar (Figure 2). The roof of your mouth is called the *hard palate.* When you close your mouth, your tongue touches the fixed roof. The soft, fleshy part in the back of the roof is called the *soft palate.* The nasal cavity is located just above the hard palate. If you keep your mouth closed and breathe out, the air flows through the nasal cavity and the nose. The back part of the mouth that connects with your throat area is called the *pharynx.* It is a little tube that connects the mouth with the *esophagus,* which takes food down into your system.

Various head cavities act as sounding boards for tone. We will mention these parts as they are needed for our work. Resonance of the sounds you produce is very important to ventriloquism.

In describing how to use your vocal mechanism, we will concentrate on three things. First is your energy source for sound, the lungs. You must think about proper breathing to get the most out of your voice. Next we will consider articulation and the importance of producing each syllable of a word distinctly, then joining all the words to make clearly audible sentences. Finally, we will discuss simulation, which will help you imitate sounds without the use of your lips, in some cases, and to create sounds that appear to be far away.

Take a Deep Breath

Everyone breathes. What could be more automatic? But many people have breathing problems. Some residents of large cities or towns may breathe with difficulty without even realizing it. The air is sometimes filled with pollutants. When work or play or bad weather keeps us indoors we don't get a chance to fill our lungs with clean air. Poor posture and smoking also inhibit good breathing. We may be wrong in thinking that we are breathing correctly, even though we don't seem to be having trouble. Since vocal sounds are produced by the movement of air in the larynx, we, as ventriloquists, must be very concerned about proper breathing. The ventriloquist must be able to breathe for two voices, which change rapidly from one to another.

Here is a simple breathing test that will tell you if you are taking in enough air. Place your right hand flat against your chest about eight inches below your chin. Place your left hand four inches below the right, also with your palm flat and fingers together. Breathe in gently through your nose, mouth closed. Hold your breath for a few seconds; then breathe out through your nose again. Did either of your hands move? If your right hand moved in toward your chest as you exhaled, it is a sign that you are an "upper chest" breather. Your chest is not getting all the air it can handle. This is the most common breathing problem, and you will be able to correct it easily.

Let's take a quick look at the respiratory system so you can understand what happens when you breathe. The object is to get air into the lungs. As you inhale, the diaphragm, located between your chest and your abdomen, moves down to enlarge your chest cavity. As the cavity gets bigger, the air pressure in the space around the lungs decreases, so that the pressure of the outside air is greater than the pressure inside your chest. This difference in pressure causes the outside air to rush into your system to fill your lungs. It happens quite naturally and you never have to stop to think about it.

When you exhale, the diaphragm returns to its normal position and the pressure of the air inside the chest forces the excess air to leave the lungs. Air enters your nose through the two nostrils and passes through the nasal passage. Tiny mucous membranes act as filters to keep out dust and some bacteria. People who breathe through their mouths do not have this protection. The air then goes into the throat (pharynx) and down to the larynx on its way to your lungs. Between the throat and the larynx is a small flap called the *epiglottis*. This flap opens and closes at the proper times to prevent food from entering the windpipe when you eat and to allow air to flow in and out of your body properly when you breathe. People are usually quite impressed when a ventriloquist appears to drink liquid and produce sound at the same time. In fact, the epiglottis will not allow this to happen.

While learning your ventriloquial skill, take time to improve your breathing. Try the test described earlier. With both hands on your chest, palms against your body, inhale slowly, trying to keep the upper chest as rigid as possible. It should not move when you exhale. Keep your head straight, and as you exhale whisper the sound of "aah." If your head tilts too far upward, you strain your larynx. If your head tilts too far forward, the sound will come out muffled. Try these exercises:

1. Stand straight with your hands at your sides, feet slightly apart. Swing both hands and arms forward as you gently inhale. As you exhale, swing both arms back. On the forward swing you will see that your chest expands to let you take in more air. Try this a few times before the next exercise.

2. Inhale gently and raise your arms over your head. Hold your breath and slowly count "1-2-3-4-5." Bring your arms down, and as you exhale whisper the sound "aah" again. Hold the "aah" for five beats. Breathe normally for a while and then repeat the exercise.

3. After a few days you can start to increase the number of beats to ten, then fifteen and twenty. You will gradually become more comfortable, and you will find that you can hold your breath longer each day. Vary the whispered sound from "aah" to "oo," "ee," and "oh." Tighten your stomach muscles a bit when you inhale. If you work in front of a mirror you can watch to see that your chest does not move too much. Pretend that air is going into your stomach.

Proper breath control will help you in more ways than just improving your ventriloquism. You'll find that you will be able to speak more clearly, sing, and even sleep better. It is important to mention here that smoking will definitely impair your natural breathing and can ruin your vent technique.

Put on a Happy Face

Now it's time to get down to work. Smile! Look in your mirror for a moment and concentrate on your lips. Don't look so serious—smile a few times. Keep the smile and separate your lips so that they are a quarter of an inch apart. Your teeth should be parted. Keep your jaw as rigid as possible. While still smiling, say "ah."

You don't need to move your lips or your jaw for that simple sound. Repeat it a few times, always checking the mirror in front of you. Try the sound again, but this time sing it and hold the tone for a while: "Aahhhh."

Relax. Can you duplicate the same happy lip and jaw position and repeat the exercise? Good.

Most sounds can be made without the use of the lips. The simple consonants need no lip movement. All the sounds that need the lips are called *labial* sounds. Some *plosives,* such as the sounds of *p* and *b,* are made by putting the lips together. The air is exhaled against the lips, causing them to "pop" when the sound is made. Sounds such as *f, v,* and *w* also need the lips.

The easiest sounds to make with no lip movement are the simple vowel sounds. If you can, prop a small mirror in front of you while you practice; it will be easier to work with than a wall mirror. Smile again and resume your position with lips apart and teeth almost touching. You are going to try the five vowel sounds of *a, e, i, o,* and *u.* Start by saying *a:*

ay . . . ay . . . ay

This sound requires no lip movement. Whisper it a few times so that you don't strain your voice. Then say it aloud a few times. Do this with all the vowel sounds. Try the next one, *e:*

ee . . . ee . . . ee

Watch the mirror, and keep a tight jaw. Whisper the sound, say it aloud, and then do the first two together, *a-e:*

ay . . . ee . . . ay . . . ee . . . ay . . . ee

Repeat with *i:*

eye . . . eye . . . eye

Whisper it, say it aloud, and combine the three, *a-e-i:*

ay . . . ee . . . eye . . . ay . . . ee . . . eye

Do the same with *o:*

oh . . . oh . . . oh

Pronounce the *u* by saying "you" or "ee-oo" with the emphasis on the "oo" sound:

you . . . you . . . you

To keep the sounds flowing, take a good breath before you start; then sing the vowels:

ay . . . ee . . . eye . . . oh . . . you

Keep the same happy facial expression and keep your lips slightly parted. Watch your jaw. Remember not to move it.

The illustration (Figure 3) shows the normal position of your lips when you are speaking naturally. As a performer, your natural speech should be clear and distinct. As a ventriloquist, it should be quite different from the speech of your figure. When he speaks, your face will be immobile except for your smile and your eye movements. When you speak, he will be motionless and your lips and features will be more alive. To help create this difference in your early practice sessions, speak the vowels in

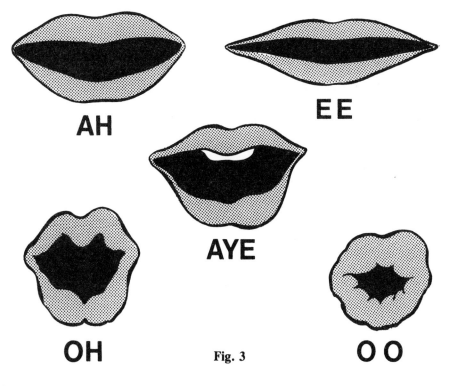

AH

EE

AYE

OH Fig. 3 **O O**

your normal voice, with relaxed jaw and exaggerated lip movements, enunciating every sound with care.

Exercise with the vowels two different ways. First do the "still lip" vowel sound with no lip movement. Then repeat it in a normal manner. Go on to the next sound quickly, doing the same thing, so that you can get in the habit of speaking with and without lip movement at will. At the moment, do not worry about changing your voice. We'll discuss this later. The following exercises will help you.

ay *(no lip movement; tight jaw)*
ay *(lips wide apart)*

ee *(no lip movement)*
ee*(lips separated slightly, as when you smile)*

eye *(no lip movement)*
eye *(lips only slightly apart)*

oh *(no lip movement)*
oh *(lips almost in a circle)*

you *(no lip movement)*
you *(lips pursed as though you were kissing)*

Change rapidly from one to the next. Vary the pattern from time to time. Try all the sounds with no lip movement; then do them again in your normal voice. Try them backward and forward, in and out of order. Use your imagination to come up with variations. Add a few other sounds such as:

oo . . . ow . . . aw . . . eh . . . ah

In order not to get too tired, whisper them at first; then make them audible; then sing them.

To keep a good space between the teeth, some people like to place a flat ice-cream stick between their teeth while practicing so they can get the feel of keeping their teeth gently apart. Try the exercise while holding a pencil between your teeth. Then try it without the extra help. Remember the key factors: keep your lips apart, hold your teeth apart or gently touching, smile, keep a rigid jaw, and practice. After all this, practice some more.

Change Your Voice

Many teachers have tried to describe in print the method used for changing your voice, but it is difficult to do. You will find that the correct sound for your new partner's voice will evolve through basic trial and error. A book can only offer you guidelines. You have just seen that the vowel sounds can be made without using the lips or moving the jaw. You have practiced these sounds for a while and you know that they are relatively easy to produce. Now try the exercises again, but this time with a difference in the tone of your voice. Vary from your normal tone to a nasal one. Pinch your nose and say the vowels quickly. The sound will be an exaggerated nasal one. Now try it this way. Touch the tip of your tongue to your upper teeth. Slide your tongue back toward the soft palate at the roof of your mouth. The underside of the tongue tip should go back as far as it comfortably can. Say:

ay . . . ee . . . eye . . . oh . . . ee-oo

You will notice that the sound is now diffused. The difference is not too great at present but the tone is definitely changed.

Now try it again by raising the tone an octave. Here is how to do this. Sing the first line of "The Star-Spangled Banner":

Oh, say, can you see . . .

The word *say* and the word *see* are an octave apart. Practice singing the two words as "ay" and "ee." Try the "ay" in your normal tone, then the "ee" with the tongue in the diffused position. You will be singing the "ee" in the higher octave. Now try all the vowel sounds in the higher octave. Then speak the same sounds rather than singing them.

Another trick for changing your voice is by adding pressure. Tighten up your diaphragm as you practice the vowel sounds. Once again your voice has changed. It is somewhat squeezed. Practice the vowel sounds with both your regular and your changed voice. Soon you will find that the second voice will come more naturally.

Vent Alphabet

The vent alphabet has no labial or plosive sounds. Next you are going to recite the alphabet with tight lip control, leaving out the tough letters. Practice each letter with a mirror on hand, as you did with the vowel sounds.

a—You have already practiced this vowel, pronounced "ay."

b—This is a labial, plosive sound. We will *leave it out* for now.

c—Touch your teeth together gently and push air out to produce a slight hissing sound followed by the vowel sound "ee" as in the word *see*. In reciting the alphabet, *c* is pronounced this way, but in some words, such as *cat,* it is pronounced like the letter *k.*

d—Place the tip of your tongue against the upper palate at the point where the palate meets the teeth. Add the "ee" sound for the sound of "dee."

e—You have already practiced this vowel, pronounced "ee."

f—This is a labial sound. *We will omit it.*

g—The soft *g* is made with the teeth touching very gently as the air is forced out, the tongue touching the upper palate. Try it once; then try it again with the teeth a bit apart. Add the "ee" for "gee." The hard *g,* as in the word *great,* is made without the teeth. The back of the tongue touches the soft palate for this sound.

h—In the alphabet this is pronounced "aych." In the word *how,* it is merely a rush of air being exhaled. For this exercise pronounce "ay" and then add the "ch" sound as in the word *child*. The accent is on the "ay" sound. You may try to add a *t* so that you do not purse your lips too much: "ate-ch." Blend the two sounds together as one.

i—You have already practiced *i,* pronounced "eye."

j—As in the soft *g* sound, the tongue touches the hard palate almost like a *d*. Use the "ay" ending for "jay."

k—This sound is made without the tongue. It comes from the soft palate and it is pronounced like the *c* in *car*. Add "ay" for "kay."

l—Here is a two-part sound. Use the "eh" sound with a bit of breath added. The second part is made with the tongue

26

touching the inside of the top front teeth: "eh-ll," blended to "ell."

m—This is a labial. *Leave it out.*

n—The tongue touches the top of the front teeth but it arches and flattens against the hard palate. In the alphabet, *n* is pronounced "eh-n," blended to "ehn." Alone, it is the first sound in such words as *noodle* and *noon.*

o—Another vowel, "oh."

p—This is a plosive; *leave it out.*

q—This is a combination of the *k* and *u* sounds: "kee-you," blended to form "cue."

r—Say "ah," moving your tongue up toward the upper palate to produce the rolling sound of the *r:* "ah-r," "are."

s—Put your teeth together and hiss as you expel the air: "ss." Add the "eh" in front of the hiss for the "ess" sound.

t—The tongue gently touches the hard palate at the spot where it meets the top of the front teeth. It hardly touches the palate, making just a tiny pop. It is a soft sound. Add the "ee" for "tee." In the word *this,* the air flow needs a bit more pressure. The tongue action is not as gentle as in the word *too.*

u—Another vowel, "ee-oo." When you pronounce it, do not purse your lips.

v, w—These are labials. *Leave them out* for this exercise.

x—Pronounce this as "eks." It is an "eh" plus a *k* sound plus an "ess."

y—Pronounce this "oo" and "eye" blended together for "oo-eye." In such words as *you* or *yes,* the sound is made like the alphabet letter *u.*

z—Make a hard *s* sound like the buzzing of a bee. The teeth should be touching as the air is forced through them.

Now go through the twenty-letter alphabet as written here, *without* the labial or plosive sounds that have been omitted. Try them again in a changed voice. These twenty letters are pronounced as:

ay . . . see . . . dee . . . ee . . . gee . . . aych . . . eye . . .
jay . . . kay . . . ell
ehn . . . oh . . . cue . . . are . . . ess . . . tee . . . ee-oo . . .
eks . . . oo-eye . . . zee

You can come up with many words and phrases that do not use the six letters you left out. After rehearsing the vent alphabet in front of your mirror, without lip movement, try a few of these practice phrases:

It's a nice night, isn't it?
It's late already.
Are you rushing out?

A few tongue twisters will help you practice your enunciation and remind you not to trip over your words:

Red leather readers . . .
Real literary leisure . . .
Stick a stick across a stick . . .
She sells sea shells at the sea shore . . .

You can now recite the vowels and consonants of the vent alphabet without lip movement. It's time to try a few of the easy numbers:

oo-un . . . too . . . three . . . sicks . . . ate . . . nine . . . ten
. . . thirteen
sicksteen . . . nineteen . . . too-un-tee

Work on the "three" and "thirteen." Allow your tongue to touch your teeth and hard palate at the point where they join. A slight push will give you the hiss for the "th" sound. Practice a few numbers in simple sentences:

One and one are two.
Two and two and another two are six.
Three sticks are sitting on the stage.
I saw six soldiers.
"Are you hungry?" "No, I ate at eight."
Nine naughty dogs chased nineteen naughty cats.
Ten and three are thirteen.

Watch for lip movement; keep a rigid jaw; and remember to smile. Make up your own simple sentences and practice them.

How are you, Harry?
Who is here tonight?
How did you get that stain?
I sat on an egg.

3

SUBSTITUTE SOUNDS

With the simple alphabet and number exercises, you can now pronounce most sounds without any lip movement or change in your facial expression. The six letters we left out of the alphabet represent additional sounds and require a bit more work. You will not reproduce these sounds exactly, but the listener will hear what he expects to hear. You will, in fact, use some vocal magic to create the illusion of saying the proper sound. This is done by using a substitute.

Letter *W*

Let us start with a simple substitute for the letter *w*. The normal method of producing the *w* sound requires that you purse your lips as though you were saying "oo." You know that the simple "oo" sound can be made without lip movement if you concentrate on it. To create the sound closest to the *w*, you place the "oo" in front of the word you want to use. As an example, we will take the five famous *w* questions; who, what, when, where, and why.

The easiest is the word *who*, which is pronounced with an *h* in front of the "oo." It sounds like "hoo." In all the other words you will add the "hoo" preceding the rest of the word. For example, *where* is pronounced "oo-air." To avoid making a two-syllable word out of it, blend the sounds closer together by using more breath. Say "hoo-air," whispering the *h* rather than sounding it. This will help the blend. Try some of these:

29

When (oo-en) will you get there?
What (oo-ot) did you say?

Why (oo-eye) are you there?
What (oo-ot) do you want?
Who (hoo) is that?

Practice some of these words while working with your mirror:

witch	wheat
water	warm
words	wine
waiter	winter
weather	

Now try using some of these jokes, changing your voice with a bit of pressure and keeping a still lip. The letter *V* represents the ventriloquist, and you will use your normal voice for these lines. The *F* stands for the figure, and for this you will use your ventriloquial second voice.

V: Last night I had the audience in the aisles.
F: Which way were they going?

V: You mustn't yawn in the audience's face.
F: Why not? They started it.

F: I told her that her stockings were wrinkled.
V: Then why was she angry?
F: She wasn't wearing any.

In the alphabet, *w* is pronounced as "dubble-you" and uses a *b* sound. Do not add this to your alphabet until you have studied the *b*.

Letter *F*

The normal sound of the letter *f* is made by brushing your lower lip against your upper teeth. In your normal way say, "feeling fine." Watch your lips in the mirror. Since the vent voice does not allow lip movement, you need another way to make the same sound. Vents use several different methods to produce a substitute for *f*. I will describe two methods and you can see which one suits you best. Remember that you must always choose the most comfortable way of pronouncing all your lines.

With lips apart, take in some air. Press the tip of your tongue gently against the base of your upper teeth. The sound you will make is similar to the "th" in the word *think*. The alphabet letter is pronounced "eff." Add the sound "eh" in front of the "th" to give you "eth." At first, the word may sound a bit flat, so gradually soften the "th" until you barely pronounce it (Figure 4).

The most common usage of the letter *f* is at the beginning of a word such as *feel*. Make the "th" sound barely audible while you pronounce the rest of the word louder and with more air: "th-eel." The accent is on the "eel." This technique will come to you with some practice. Try a few of these words, accenting the underlined part of the word, rather than the "th" sound:

f<u>un</u>ny thunny	<u>finger</u>
<u>foo</u>lish = thoolish	<u>flash</u>-
	light
<u>fee</u>ling = theeling	<u>fate</u>
<u>fire</u>	<u>fi</u>ckle
<u>fix</u>	fl<u>y</u>ing

When it is used in the middle of a word, the *f* is pronounced with the same "th" sound, but the emphasis is on the beginning and end of the word so that the *f* is almost completely unpronounced. A word like *infant* becomes "in-th-ant." Now try a few of these sentences with your vent voice and no lip movement. Remember to use your mirror.

He had an infant (<u>in</u>-th-<u>ant</u>) son.
Filling (th-<u>illin</u>-g) stations offer (<u>aw</u>ther) gas.
Fry an egg for Francis.
Feel free to fire away.

Now add a few *w* sounds:

What do you want, Fred (thred)?
Where is the fire?
When will you feel okay?
Where did you find a whole wheat sandwich?

It's time now to alternate the sounds of your regular and second vent voices.

> F: His wife eats crackers.
> V: What's wrong with that?
> F: Fire-crackers?

> V: What time is it?
> F: It's very easy to tell.
> V: How?
> F: There's a sundial out in the hall.
> V: That's silly. It's dark in the hall.
> F: So take a flashlight.

Alternate F Sound

This method of pronouncing f is used by Howard Olson, a teacher of ventriloquism in Madison, Wisconsin. Olson uses a "ch" sound for the f. The sound is like the German pronunciation of the final sound in *Bach*. If you think of something disgusting, you might say, "Yuch."

In English, we do not use this sound at all. To produce it, you have to force air through a small opening in the back of your throat. As the air hits the throat, the sound is made by friction. Put your head back and say "aah." Bring your head back again and, keeping your mouth open, say "aka . . . aka." Concentrate on the k sound and you'll feel your throat closing between the two a sounds. If you tighten up your throat again as you pronounce the $k,$ you should get the sound we're looking for. Try this line:

> It's foolish (choo-lish).

The "ch" sound should be softer than the rest of the word.

If you learn both methods of pronouncing the substitute $f,$ you have the advantage of being able to alternate them, fitting the best sound into your scripts for more realistic f's. For normal use, choose the one that is more comfortable for you.

Letter *V*

The *v* sound is produced very much like the *f* sound. For the letter *f*, you touched your tongue to the inside of your top teeth very gently. This time you must press harder and get the sound of "th" as used in the word *these*. You will notice a slight tingle or vibration as you practice. Always accent the rest of the word when you use a *v* or an *f* (Figure 4). Try a few words:

aviation = ay-thee-<u>ay</u>-shun
very nice = th<u>ery</u> nice
evening = <u>ee</u>-then-ing *(blend into a smooth sound)*

Try a few of these sentences. Accent the underlined part of the word.

How <u>are</u> you this <u>e</u>vening?
That was <u>very</u> nice.
Av<u>iation</u> is growing very quickly.
Are you <u>lea</u>ving now?
Let's have a conver<u>sation</u>.
<u>E</u>verything is okay.

Add a few *f* and *w* words:

Wouldn't it be fun to have a conversation?
When did you feel I was vague?

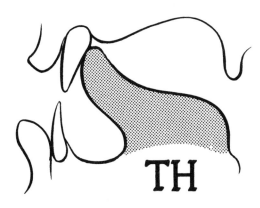

Fig. 4 A substitute for the letter F. More pressure of the tongue creates a V sound.

Change your voices with this dialogue:

> F: Victor is very sick.
> V: What's wrong with him?
> F: He thinks he's a chicken.
> V: You ought to take him to a hospital.
> F: We would—only we need the eggs.

Alternate *V* Sound

As in the case of the letter *f*, there is an alternate way to create a substitute *v* sound. Howard Olson teaches the "ch" sound for both letters, but in the case of the *v*, the pressure in the throat is a bit greater, producing more vibration. Olson would use

It's all oh-ch-er = over
ch-ery nice = very nice

He describes the sound as a soft cough combined with a soft letter *g*.

Before you go any further, take time to go over the earlier lessons in order to keep everything you are learning in the proper perspective. Go back now and do some of the breathing exercises. Sing and whisper the various sounds. Try the vowels again until they are easy to do in front of a mirror. Remember to keep your lips apart and your jaw rigid. Keep your teeth apart and allow the air to flow in and out freely as you speak. Try to hold your breath for longer periods. Now try the vent alphabet again, but this time add the *f* ("eth") and *v* ("thee").

Letter *M*

The normal sound of *m* is made with a hum, "mmm," while the lips are held together. There are several ways to produce a substitute. In many cases when a word or phrase is easily recognizable, a simple *n* sound will pass for an *m*. In most cases, however, you need a better and richer sound. We are going to use the sound of "ng" as used in a word ending. Say the word *going*. Now say "ungah." Figure 5 shows how the tongue flattens

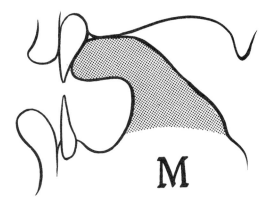

Fig. 5 Tongue flattens against hard palate.

out behind the top teeth. Once more, try "ungah." Say "eng." In
both cases try not to sound the *g*. Now say the word *tongue*. The
"ng" sound in all of these words will sound like the *m* if you can
flatten it out a little. When it is used in conjunction with other
parts of a word you will see how it works. Here is an excellent
example used by Bob Neller in his tape teaching method.

Say the word *tomato*. Now say it again as "tongue-nato." In
the vent voice, blend the words together, dropping the second *n*
sound. The sound will be that of "tongue-ato." If your tongue is
against the hard palate it will sound like "tomato." Do not pause
between the word parts. It must sound as though it were all one
word. The word *mother* is made with the sounds "eng" and
"other" blended to "eng-other." Leave out the *e* and you will
have the *m* sound. Try it for these sounds:

Mary = ng-ary
lamb = la-ng

Since everyone is familiar with this next phrase it is easy to
cheat a little and use *n* for the first word and "ng" for the end of
the sentence, as in:

N-ary had a little la-ng. = Mary had a little lamb.

Accent the "ary" sound.

When a phrase is familiar to your audience, they will accept

35

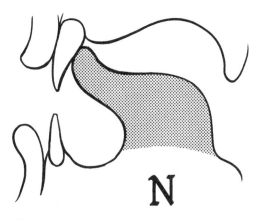

Fig. 6 Can often pass for the letter M.

the *n*, but you must still remember to place the emphasis on the rest of the word (Figure 6).

Ladies and <u>gentle</u>-nen.

The accent on "gentle" will allow the *n* to go unnoticed.

The Great Lester used to pronounce the *m* by touching his tongue to the inside of his upper lip. This takes a good deal of practice and is most effective. You should have perfect lip control for this method. Another method is to place your tongue on the floor of your mouth just below your lower teeth. This allows the back part of the tongue to hit the soft palate. Try both methods or all three until you find a comfortable pronunciation. I suggest the first method, for ·it is learned most quickly. Alternate the "n" and "ng" sounds for some of these sentences. Then try Lester's method and see which is more comfortable for you.

Don't mention it to me.
I'll sing for mother (ng-other).
There were ten men (ng-en) on the street.
Mary had a little lamb.
How many times?
Ladies and gentlemen, may I have a word with you?
In the merry (ng-erry) month (n-onth) of May.
If I had my (ny) way.
I like tomato (tongue-ato) soup.

Let's try a few dialogues in two voices.

> V: What are you going to sing?
> F: If I had my way.
> V: That's nice.
> F: If I had my way, I'd go home.

> V: Can you spell Washington?
> F: State or man?
> V: State.
> F: Ess-tee-ay-tee-ee.

> F: I got a ticket for driving twenty miles an hour.
> V: Twenty miles an hour is not illegal.
> F: On the sidewalk?

Add the letter *m* to the alphabet and go through it once or twice: "ell," "ng," "ehn." With some practice, you will be able to make the sound without even using the tip of your tongue. The back of your tongue will easily hit the soft palate and produce the sound for you. Here are a few *m* words for extra practice:

many	mind	Margaret
miles	mingle	immediate
Mary	more	mention
men	time	mother
marriage		

Letter *B*

A psychological factor is involved in learning and producing this sound. If you firmly believe that you are saying a *b*, it will sound like a *b*. As you produce the substitute sound, you must *think* of the *b* sound. If you first convince yourself, your listener will hear what you want him to hear. It is the same psychology used by magicians who pretend to do one thing while actually doing something else. Let's see how the magic of *b* works.

Several sounds can be used to pass as *b*. One is the letter *d*. The substitute *d* must be made with your tongue flattened against

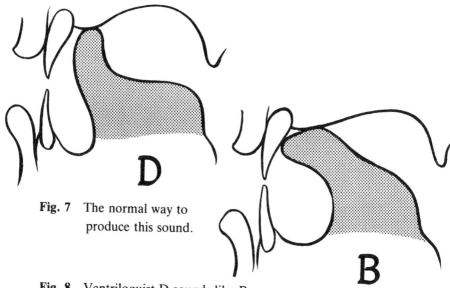

Fig. 7 The normal way to produce this sound.

Fig. 8 Ventriloquist D sounds like B.

the upper palate (Figure's 7 and 8). Say the word *beautiful*. Now, without lip movement and concentrating on the *b* sound, pronounce it "dee-oo-tee-thul." Repeat this a bit more rapidly, with the accent on the "oo" sound, thinking of the *b*.

Try the word *bottle*. If you merely said it with a *d*, it would have the flat sound of "dottle." But if you think of the letter *b* and accent the last part, "ottle," you will hear it as "bottle." The phrase "a bottle of soda" would be spoken as "a dottle o' soda." Note that we left out the *f*. The audience is so familiar with the phrase that they will believe they heard the *b* and the *f*. Just some more vocal magic.

The Great Lester advocated placing the tip of the tongue against the inside of the upper lip to produce the *d*. You can try this method, but remember to watch for lip movement in the mirror. If there is too much movement one way, try another.

A second way to produce the *b* sound—another old vaudeville method—is to use the hard *g* as in *guy*. The use of the *g* must be carefully planned and alternated with the *d* sound so that you don't get the common "gottle o' geer" for "bottle of beer." You might say "a gottle o' deer," provided the accents are properly placed. The *g* would be pronounced very softly and the "eer" accented at the end. A quiet *g* can be used occasionally when the sound of *b* must be used more than once in a sentence.

A third alternative uses the *v* substitute, so that you get "thottle" or "theer." Now the phrase would be "a dottle o' theer," which, if said rapidly, is quite close to the perfect sound.

With three alternatives, you can choose a combination for yourself and pick out the one that is most comfortable for you. The *d* is the first choice and will probably be used most often. The *v* and *g* will be used as fill-ins. Play with some of these and try one or more of the *b* substitutes. Remember to *think b* as you say them.

> bread and butter = dred and thutter
> *or* gred and dutter
> *or* thread and dutter
>
> hamburgers and a bottle of beer = han-dur-gers and a dottle o' theer
> very bashful = thery dash-thul
> a cute baby and his bottle = a cute day-thee and his thottle

Here is another trick that you can use to help confuse the listener. Let us say that you want your figure to say "I bought some beans." Rather than trip over two *b* sounds so close to each other, you can adapt your script and plant the idea in the listener's mind this way:

> V: Were you at the grocery?
> F: Yes, I was.
> V: What did you buy?
> F: Beans (deans).
> V *(Repeats the word properly):* Beans?
> F: That's what I bought (dought).
> V: What did you buy?
> F: I bought (dought) some (sung) beans (theans).

Here are some more double gags you can use with your normal (V) and changed (F) voices.

> V: How's your brother?
> F: Which one (oo-ich oo-un)?
> V: The one who died.
> F: Much better (ng-uch thetter), thank you.

F: I just ate ten hamburgers (han-durgers).
V: You ate ten hamburgers, alone?
F: No, with mustard (ng-ustard).

Add the *b* to the alphabet. Try it two ways:

ay . . . dee . . . cee
or ay . . . thee . . . cee

Go through the alphabet again. Add the *b, f, m, v,* and *w.* The *w* may sound like "duddle-you" or "duggle-you" or "duthel-you." You will find that the *g* sound is the most effective.

Letter *P*

Once more you are presented with several choices to help you find the right *p* sound. You may use a combination of methods, alternating them to make your sentences more comfortable. First, try it this way. Touch the tip of your tongue to the soft palate near the back of your top teeth. Pop the *t* sound gently as you pronounce your words (Figures 9 and 10).

Teter = Peter
tlease = please
oh-ten = open
attlesauce = applesauce

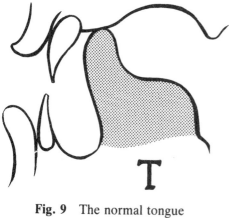

Fig. 9 The normal tongue position for T.

Fig. 10 Flatten the tongue for the P sound.

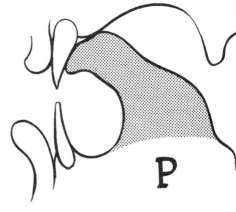

As an alternative, the letter *k* is often used softly to sound like a *p*.

Oken (open) the door.
Klease (please) don't say no.

Bob Neller advocates the use of a combination of the *k* and *t* sounds. He uses "attlesauce" and "acklesauce," and by combining both sounds, using the tip and the back of the tongue, creates a sound that is almost perfect.

You might combine both sounds in the words that have two *p* sounds close together:

Pick it up = tick it uk
or kick it ut

Paul Stadelman used to leave out the *p* altogether in a word like *open.* He would say, "O'en the door," leaving an ever-so-slight pause after the *o.* Since the audience is familiar with the word and the phrase, they accept the fact that it was, in fact, pronounced. More magic psychology. Try some of these sentences:

Please pay attention (thleese tay attention).
It was a pleasant party.
Pick it up.
Keep up with the times.
May I have a piece of paper?
His name is Peter. He's a very fine person.
I like pickles, upside down.
He was upside down at the door.
Money is fine for poor people.

Practice . . . kractice . . . tracktice. The tongue must make a small pop as it curls to hit the roof of the mouth. Try not to make the *t* very flat. Change your voice a little for these practice exercises.

F: Last night I dreamt I was flying.
V: Why don't you sleep on your back?
F: What? And fly upside down?

F: He was killed seventy-five years ago in a parachute jump.

V: They didn't have parachutes seventy-five years ago.
F: I know. That's how he got killed.

F: The President called me yesterday.
V: What did he say?
F: I didn't hear a word.
V: Why not?
F: I don't have a telephone.

F: I wish I had a nickel for every girl I kissed.
V: What would you do with the money?
F: I'd buy a pack of gum.

Go back to your mirror and try some of these words:

winding	mending
finding	bending
fending	binding
depending	minding
vending	pending

Now you are ready for the test. Read the first paragraph of your daily newspaper with no lip movement or jaw movement. Read slowly and clearly, as every word must be read with some expression. Use your substitutes when you need them. A tape recorder at your side would help a great deal. Pretend that you are a newscaster broadcasting the television news. Glance at the paper and then read the line to the mirror; this is a very good exercise for things to come.

At this point we will go back to your vent voice. You have been practicing with a second voice that has been diffused, or under pressure, or an octave higher. You must now go back to all the dialogues and flavor them with a further change of voice. If you are speaking in a normal tone, your figure (F) will be speaking somewhat louder. Speak the words of your own speech (V) carefully and slowly, and speak the figure's lines a little more quickly and less precisely. Now do it the other way. You speak quickly and allow the figure to speak more slowly.

To create the difference between the sounds, you must try to vary the tone, pitch, pressure, speed, and personality of the two

Monsieur Brunard, whose real name is Dick Bruno, was originally a musician. He was greatly impressed by the works of John Cooper and began learning ventriloquism from books. After a meeting with the Great Lester he decided to become a full-time vent. During World War II he and Joe Flip toured around the world with the act. He still works and teaches ventriloquism in Florida.

voices. As an added exercise, you might try to mimic various types of accents, such as clipped British, heavy Russian, nasal French, flowing Spanish or Italian. Try speaking as though you were from one of those countries and you were learning English. Monsieur Brunard created a perfect act by speaking in a heavy French accent, while his figure speaks in the slurred tones of an American city kid. The choice of language can be different. Try speaking in proper, careful grammar while your figure talks slang. The difference created in speech patterns will assist you in creating the illusion of two separate people.

4

CHOOSING YOUR PARTNER

It is unfortunate, but at the time of this writing, there are very few inexpensive practice figures on the market. Pelham Puppets of Marlborough, England, makes a simple vent puppet that has a headstick control. The figure is about twenty-four inches tall with cloth body and legs. The figure has no arms, so you must use your own hand in the sleeve. This gives the figure a realistic arm. A few dolls on the market look like vent characters. These are good for very little children, but do not have headsticks. The heads are motionless, the mouths controlled by pulling a string in the back of the neck.

The most reasonable professional figures are molded from a plaster cast and made of wood fiber or fiberglass. They are lightweight, quite good, and will last for many years. The back of the head has a small door cut out of it, hidden under the wig, so that the mechanism can be reached in case of trouble. Molded figures are made in two parts. The movements are put into the front section and the back of the head is added later.

Hand-carved figures are the most desirable for the working performer. These are carved to specifications from sturdy basswood or pine. No two are alike. Most of the performers you see on television use hand-carved figures, but very few people do this type of carving. Some of the famous hand carvers are Mack, Marshall, Pinxy, Finis, Coates, Turner, MacElroy, and Olson. Most of these are names of the past.

Frank Marshall in his studio. Marshall carved many of the most famous American vent figures. He worked for Charlie Mack and after Mack died took over the business. Since Marshall's death, his figures have become collectors' items. (Photo courtesy of Mark Wade from the Vent Haven Museum collection.)

For the beginner, the little boy or girl figure is best. This figure can be given any type of character you need, any type of voice you want to create, and you can dress it in clothing to fit the personality you choose. If you cannot afford a figure at first, you can use a good puppet until you learn your craft (see Chapter 6).

Ventriloquial Figures

In the classic picture of the ventriloquist, a human-looking wooden boy or girl sits on the ventriloquist's knee. The "knee figure" is generally a wise little character who is expected to talk back to the ventriloquist with quips and smart-aleck remarks. The classic "cheeky boy" figure was popularized in England. This type of character can use any voice, and his personality allows you to use many kinds of scripts. Terri Rogers is most successful with her cheeky boy, "Shorty," a nasty but cute character who always tries to embarrass her. Other figures include such novelties as an old man or old woman, talking objects, and animal puppets (see Chapter 6).

Terri Rogers, England's most popular modern ventriloquist. She and her Davenport figure, Shorty, have done television and club work and are best known for hilarious "cabaret" performances.

Since the character to be developed must appear to be real, vent figures often have many lifelike moving features. The mouth movement is most important, and there are two kinds. One, called the "slot mouth," is the most common and provides good stage visibility. The section below the upper lip has slits on either side of the mouth, cut through to the lower jaw. The entire lower section moves when the figure speaks.

In another type of mouth movement the lower lip portion of the mouth is covered with a soft material such as doeskin. There are no slits on the side. The mouth can be made to move only as far as the chin line. The lever for the mouth, called a *control*, is set on a headstick. This means the head is separate from the body of the doll. The stick is like a broom handle, wide enough to hold with four fingers, so that your thumb or index finger can manipulate the mouth control.

Most figures have a trigger mechanism that pulls a cord going into the head of the doll. The cord is made of nylon, leather, or sturdy piano wire, for it must be able to withstand the constant pressure of movement. The other end of the cord goes to the mouth and is attached inside the head on a tight spring. The spring enables the mouth to close by itself when the tension is relaxed. Learning to control the mouth is quite simple. To open the mouth you merely press the lever. You keep your thumb on the lever to control the speed with which the mouth closes. The ventriloquist cannot allow the mouth to spring back into place by itself, or it will click with the sound of a trap closing. The mouth of your figure should move smoothly. Should it stick, a bit of vaseline or a spray of silicone will keep the sides from rubbing.

The hand holding the post can also manipulate the head so that it turns from side to side. It can tip forward or lean back at the whim of the ventriloquist.

Some vent figures have moving glass eyes controlled by another lever on the headstick. This control can be a side-to-side lever or a bar that can be pushed to the right or left. The eyes are connected to the lever inside the head so they can look from right to left. Most eye movements are made so that the eyes go back to the center position when the control is not being used. Some eyes are balanced so they turn when the head turns. The fingertip control is most popular, so the ventriloquist can be in full control of the movements. Eyes should be made to move slowly so their movements will be seen by everyone looking at the figure.

Many other movements are possible, but the more movements a vent figure has, the more work it is for the ventriloquist and the more parts there are to consider for repairs. In addition, for the beginner, too many movements may be distracting to you and your audience and may detract from your performance.

Mouth and eye movements are standard with most figure makers, but eyes can also be made so they wink. Each eye is controlled by its own lever, and both eye levers are generally next to one another so that both eyes can easily be closed at the same time. The eyes never close all the way, so there is no undue pressure on the springs that control the lids. Lids are generally covered with a soft material like latex or doeskin so they look natural and keep their shape. Eye parts are quite complicated to make, with many wires and pieces, and are therefore delicate. Charlie McCarthy had only a single mouth control and no extra movements. Edgar Bergen brought him to life without the gimmicks.

Often, the eyebrows can be raised by a single control that lifts both eyebrows at the same time. All the controls are on the headstick within reach of the ventriloquist's fingers. Other movements include a sneer (raising the upper lip), a stick-out tongue (made on a roller to bring it back into the mouth automatically), and wiggling ears for comic characters. Bob Neller owns a figure with more than ten moving parts.

Each lever on the headstick controls an important function.

Moving the Mouth

Even though you may not have a figure at this time, you should start learning the mouth control. For every syllable spoken by the figure, you must move the mouth. Here is an easy way to practice. Use a pencil with an eraser on top. Curl your fingers around the pencil as if it were your headstick. Your thumb must rest on top of the eraser. Figure 11 shows how this will look on an actual headstick. Lift the thumb and press it down for every syllable your figure will speak. Try a few of these sentences, hitting the eraser once for each syllable. Use your vent voice with lips apart and no jaw movement.

It's a nice night, isn't it? *(seven syllables)*
It's a nice night, isn't it?
1 2–3   4   5–6 7

Notice that movements five and six are very close to one another. Therefore you move your thumb more rapidly.

Red leather readers *(five syllables)*
Red leather readers
1   2–3   4–5

Movements two and three are short, quick movements, as are four and five.

Slowly drying dew *(two short and one longer stroke: five moves)*
Slowly drying dew
1–2   3–4   5

Practice with all the scripts and dialogue material you have

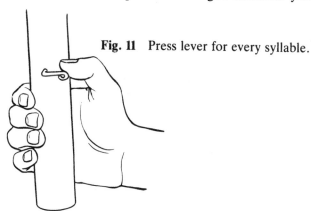

Fig. 11 Press lever for every syllable.

used so far. Break them down into syllables that would be spoken by the figure. Bob the head forward every once in a while as people do in speaking.

Mechanical Movements

As mentioned, some figures may be equipped with eye movements. These movements should be used sparingly and then only to create certain effects. If your figure has a side-to-side eye movement it can be used when the figure turns to look at you. Gently move the lever so that the eyes will move slowly as the head turns. Too quick a movement will be lost to the audience. Do not create confusion with the mechanical movements. A cute effect is created when you say something the figure doubts. He looks straight at the audience; his eyes turn toward you; and then the head turns. It is as though the figure were saying, "That can't be so." Do not actually say it. Allow the eyes to convey the message.

The eyes can move from side to side when the figure seems to be thinking about something you said. Move the first to the right, then all the way to the left, and finally back to the center. When using eye controls, keep your finger on the lever and do not allow the springs inside to bounce back by themselves; otherwise, the movements will look jerky. You want the figure to look alive and not like a mechanical doll. Practice using the lever at various speeds for unusual expressions. Check your mirror to see how they look.

Winking eyes should be used very rarely. A quick wink to a lady in the front row is cute, but only the first time you do it. Sometimes you can have the figure wink when he makes a statement everyone knows is not true. The wink tells everyone, "We know it's a joke; don't tell him." Two winkers used together can create the effect of sleep. Again, this is used only once in your show. Remember that the more moving parts you have, the more work is involved. You must concentrate on making your figure alive and entertaining, rather than on the mechanics involved.

Raising the eyebrows generally conveys surprise. Your figure's eyebrows go up when you have said something startling. To

Smiley has a right eye winker. He is a molded figure by Howard Olson. (Photo courtesy Show-Biz Services.)

make the effect more lifelike, turn the head and move the eyes after the brows have gone up and down once. Two quick movements with the eyebrows also have the effect of a greeting. These may be followed with a wink when the figure wants to flirt.

Other movements, such as wiggling ears, handshakes, and flip-up wigs, are gimmicks to be used only after you have completely established the character and personality of your partner. They are used primarily for laughs and remind the audience that this is, in fact, a doll. They do not show how clever you are as a ventriloquist and often make your figure grotesque rather than personable. I once had a figure that had an upper lip movement or sneer. When both upper and lower lips moved, the character looked quite nasty and frightened children in the audience. In the movie *Magic,* the figure has all the nasty movements, and the character is not a pleasant one, to say the least.

You will notice that I refer to your figure as though he or she were a real person. This is very important. You must consider your partner a living thing while you are working together. If you believe that the figure is real, so will your audience. The magic of suggestion builds the illusion.

51

Taking Care of Your Figure

Since ventriloquial figures are not inexpensive, you should take some time to care for them so that they will last a long time. Most figures are lifetime partners and require attention to keep them in good condition.

The clothing used for your figure should be in keeping with the personality and character on which you have decided. A sloppy boy with a "street-wise" manner should be dressed sloppily. Use good clothes but make them look used with wrinkles, a few stains, and perhaps a patch or two on the pants. The well-to-do kid will probably wear a suit and tie and a good shirt. Girl figures can be dressed in skirts or slacks and wigs. A Boy Scout or Girl Scout uniform can establish a clean-cut character.

Usually the facial expression of a figure is painted on when it is made. Most have a slight smile or eye lines that make them look real. Often the eyes are larger than life so they will be visible from the stage, but since most vents now work at closer range, this is not the general rule. The paint on the face, as well as the eyelids and delicate leather parts, must be protected from dust and scratches. I suggest that you make a bag for the head and keep it protected in the suitcase or storage box you use. Make the bag out of a terrycloth towel. If you fold the towel in half and sew up the two sides, it will make a nice bag to put over the figure's head before you put it away.

Avoid storing your figure where it is very hot. Most of the parts inside the head are glued, and glue can melt if exposed to too much heat. For instance, never leave the figure locked in its case in the hot trunk of your car during the summer months.

Keep your buddy clean. A soft, damp cloth is usually enough to wash dirt off the face. Smudges or stains can be removed with a very mild face soap. Never use an abrasive or a detergent on the face, or you will remove the paint along with the smudge. Wipe the paint dry after washing. Should the paint chip or scratch, touch it up with a soft paintbrush and the same type of paint. Ask the figure maker to tell you what type of paint was used. Latex paints are the most common.

Some figures are equipped with a head lock. This is a hook on the end of the control stick that attaches to a rubber band or eyelet on the inside of the body. The purpose of the head lock is to keep the head in position for traveling or to hold it in place when the figure is seated in a chair before a show. The head lock *must be detached* and the headstick held free while performing. Never leave the head resting inside the figure during use or the neck will rub inside the body frame and you'll be repairing it soon. When traveling, I find the best protection is to remove the head and pack it separately alongside the body. I have found that a plain fiber suitcase is the best container. It will take a good deal of abuse on planes, trains, and buses, and it is lightweight. Other cases with cloth or soft linings are also good. Make sure there is plenty of room for your figure so you do not have to jam the arms and legs inside. Foam padding around the head will prevent it from hitting the inside of the case. The case should be just large enough to accommodate your figure's body, folded in half at the waist, with room for the head and perhaps a few of your props, if you use any.

5

ANIMATION

Now is the time to bring your partner to life. Once you know that you can make it talk, you must forget that it is only a doll or a puppet. If you treat your partner as another person, your audience will do the same. Both you and your figure must react to each other's lines. The manipulation of the mouth, coordinated with the change of voices, will help create the magic. Now for the misdirection.

The mirror will tell you how well you are doing. If you have a tape recorder and can play back the voices, you can hear the changes in inflection and the difference in sound between your voice and that of your partner. Now practice with longer dialogues. Here is a good one to start with. Keep in mind that when the figure (F) speaks, the voice must change and he must speak with the same feelings as if he were real. When you (V) speak, you must do so naturally and mean what you are saying. Do not recite the lines, but speak them as though you were holding a conversation with a friend. These are not just words on paper; they are the words a real person is supposed to be speaking, and they should be spoken with expression and meaning.

> V: Hello there, what is your name?
> F *(turn headstick so he looks at you):* Willy Wackle.
> V: How do you spell it?
> F: Willy or Wackle?
> V: Wackle
> F: Easy. It's a wack and a cackle—Wackle.

V *(smile and act amused):* Where are you from, Willy?

F: Wisconsin. *(Pause) Wild* and wooly Wisconsin. *(Accent on the "wild")*

V: What do you do in Wisconsin?

F: I wash windows.

V: You're a window washer? *(Act surprised)* Where?

F: Williams Way . . . Corner of Wilson and Woolrich.

V: This is all very confusing.

F: What's so strange? I'm Willy Wackle who washes windows on Williams Way at the corner of Wilson and Woolrich in wild and wooly Wisconsin.

V: What can I say?

F: WOW!

In this script, the acting and reacting are done by the ventriloquist. Change the inflection of the words with emphasis on key words. After the first few lines, the audience will be taken in by the script itself, and the use of the *w* sounds, and will soon forget that you are a ventriloquist. The little character doing the talking will get all the credit for the amusing lines. His comedy comes from the repetition of sounds. When the figure speaks, look at him, not turning your head completely, but looking off to the side so that three-quarters of your face is seen by the audience. Choose a central spot in the audience in front of you. Make this your focal point.

Now that you have mastered the technique of having two people speaking, you should try to give the other fellow some more human qualities. When he speaks with others looking on, the figure must be conscious of the others around him, nodding at them or giving them a glance every once in a while. He shows off a bit as most people do in the same situation. From time to time, lift the headstick up and down as you turn it. No one sits immobile; people usually move about even when sitting in their seats. Your figure should do the same. You may adjust the body slightly from time to time as if he were finding a new position. These movements should be subtle and not exaggerated. If the figure is on your knee, sit in a forward position so that the movement of your knee will cause him to move gently. His legs and arms will also move a little, just the way live people do as they sit and chat with you.

When the figure is seated on your knee (Figure 12), your right arm should not move. Rest the doll on your knee, allowing your wrist to turn the headstick. Never push or pull the figure backward or forward. Your wrist and your knee action will do all the moving. When you move your knee back, the figure will tip forward. As the knee goes farther back, the figure tips farther forward. When your knee goes forward, the figure will go back, as though he were looking up.

You need not be seated to work a knee figure (see Figure 13). You might rest your foot on a chair or stool and remain standing. The animation must come from the movement of your heel and toe. If you raise your heel, the figure goes up. Pivot your toe to move your knee to the desired position.

Some ventriloquists work standing up without a chair and therefore must carry the figure in their arms. The flat seat of the body will rest on the palm of one hand, while the other hand will be inside the body on the stick. The figure's legs will be allowed to dangle. In this case, the palm of your hand must do the work of the knee, moving forward or backward to control the movements.

You might also consider using a tripod with a small flat seat on top. You should raise the tripod to the proper height, so that the figure is sitting next to you. His face should be level with yours. This may restrict some of his movements, so you must move your wrist and the headstick somewhat more to tip the figure in different directions. Choose the method that is most comfortable for you.

Try this with your figure. Have him look up at the ceiling. Move your knee forward and push the bottom of the headstick forward. The figure will tip back. You look up at the ceiling as well.

> F: Did you see anything up there?
>   *(Looks at vent)*
> V: No. What am I looking for?
> F *(looks again):* I thought I heard a plane.
> V *(looks up):* There's no plane up there.
> F *(looks up, then suddenly looks down):* Oh, oh.
> V: What is it?
> F: It's a bird.

Fig. 12

Fig. 13 Raise heel for animation.

V: *(With your other hand, take a small handkerchief from your pocket and pretend to wipe the figure's eye.)*

F: He sure knows how to aim!

Next have the figure look down. Move your knee back quite far and tip the bottom of the headstick by pulling it closer to you (Figures 14 and 15).

F *(looking down):* What's down there?

V *(looking down):* Nothing. What are you looking for?

F *(looks up, then down again):* Did you see a dollar down there? *(sits up again)*

V: No, I didn't.

F: If you see it, it's mine.

V: When did you drop it?

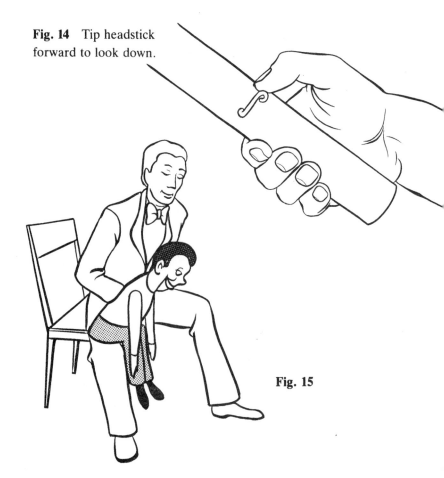

Fig. 14 Tip headstick forward to look down.

Fig. 15

F: I lost it out in the hall.

V: Then why are you looking for it here?

F: The light is much better here.

In doing this bit, you must pretend that both you and the figure are looking for the missing bill. The audience may even strain a little to see what you are looking at.

Here are some more methods to produce lifelike behavior.

Embarrassment: If your figure should become embarrassed for any reason, turn his head away from the audience and bury it in your shoulder.

Laughter: When the figure laughs, open his mouth and lift the headstick up and down in short movements. If you can move your wrist so that it moves the body, the shoulders will go up and down as well. You can make him laugh with a "ha ha ha" sound.

Coughing: You can make your partner cough by merely coughing yourself, moving the headstick in a few short, jerky movements. After his cough, say something like "Are you all right?"

Hiccupping: A "hic" sound, made by drawing in air, will serve as a hiccup.

Whispering: Every once in a while, you might have your figure whisper something to you. Make sure that the whispered lines are clear and audible.

Yawning: Open the mouth and tilt the head back. If you have winkers, close both eyes as you do this. The figure can snore once or twice. You can easily imitate the sound.

Surprise: Pull back the body and open the mouth. For a more startled response, draw the figure back toward your body quickly, as though he jumped back.

Thinking: Make your figure look up with his head turned slightly away from you. Hold him perfectly still for a moment. If you have winkers, he can close his eyes in thought.

Shame: Similar to embarrassment. Lower his head a bit and move his eyes to the corners.

Double-take: Slowly turn the head and eyes to look at you. Now turn the head to face the audience. Bring it back to the first position with a quick movement. You could tip the body sideways away from you for an extra effect.

Disbelief: Move the eyes slowly to look at you as you turn the head very slowly to face you. Gently shake the head as if to say "No." Pull the body to the side and have the figure say "Really?" Draw the word out.

Sneezing: Pull the head back while opening the mouth. As you quickly move the head forward again, say "nh-choo." Close the mouth.

> F: I'm going to sneeze.
> V: At who?
> F: At choo. *(He then sneezes again.)*
> V: Bless you.
> F: Yeah. Me too!

Crying: To make the figure appear to cry, keep his head on your shoulder and move the post up and down gently. If you can press the back of your wrist against the body, his shoulders will move at the same time. This is the same as the laughing motion.

> V: What's wrong?
> F: Everytime you sing, I cry.
> V: I wasn't singing a sad song.
> F: It's not the song that's sad, it's your singing.

In vaudeville, the team of Walters and Walters were noted for a "Crying Baby Bit," which Emily Walters performed in the act. Another ventriloquist of that era, Valentine Vox, wanted to do the same bit in his act, so he courted Emily and took her and the bit away from her husband. The new team of Vox and Walters performed the bit after they were married.

Please remember that your figure must be kept alive at all times. When you enter the stage he will move and perhaps be talking. When you leave the stage, he should be moving his head or mouth. Never let anyone in the audience, especially children, see the figure motionless. Put him away in his suitcase in private. Nothing shatters the illusion more quickly than seeing a lifeless vent figure after he has performed.

A note of caution. Never hit or shove your figure. Children will become very upset by this, since they consider your partner a real person.

6

ANYTHING CAN TALK

When my children were smaller, they claimed that I embarrassed them in restaurants when we would order clams and my empty clamshell would talk to the waiter. A simple squeeze on the top and bottom of the shell, coordinated with a little patter, and the shell spoke. With the advent of puppet shows on television, various types of talking puppets and animals have been accepted. Cigarettes, cameras, boxes, and all sorts of products came to life. The wonderful Jim Henson and his Muppets have become members of the family. Thanks to the TV puppeteers, ventriloquists were able to expand their acts by adding talking puppets of every kind. Las Vegas ventriloquist Stu Scott features an act called "Talk to the Animals" in which he uses a funny frog character and a very wise crow. I use a giant talking rabbit; Dan Ritchard uses a comical parrot; and Ken Byrd uses a jumbo crow. Mark Wade uses a squeaky pig. Almost anything can and is being used to talk to the audience.

Using Puppets

Any cloth or fur animal puppet with a movable mouth can be used for ventriloquism. The secret is in the animation so that, once again, the misdirection of the magician is applied to the puppet. To create speech for a hand puppet, you use your fingers to move the mouth. Your thumb becomes the lower lip and the other four fingers are held together to form the upper lip. While articulating, you must move its mouth, once for each syllable.

With your palm facing the floor, hold your four fingers together so that they touch. Place your thumb underneath so that it just touches the ball of your middle finger. Look in the mirror. Pretend this is the mouth of your puppet. If you separate the thumb and middle finger a few inches, the mouth will open. Close it by bringing the thumb and the fingers together again. The word *hello* will have two movements.

The puppet should move naturally. Move your wrist forward about two or three inches with each mouth movement, returning to the starting position each time. Coordinate the wrist and finger movements to resemble the snap of an alligator's jaw, with a forward flick of the wrist to punctuate each syllable. The wrist should be very loose and flexible. While you are speaking, turn your wrist so that the eyes of your puppet look into your eyes. While the figure is listening he must also move, even if only a gentle turn. If you move your wrist slightly in a figure-eight pattern, the puppet will appear to be alive even if he is silent (Figure 16).

Fig. 16   Wrist follows direction of arrows.

Cloth puppets are readily available and can be purchased in most toy and department stores. Try to select a puppet that will cover most of your arm. Make sure it has a moving mouth. Since many commercial puppets are not intended for use by the ventriloquist, you may have to add a sleeve to the bottom of the puppet to hide your arm. If you can't find a suitable toy puppet, check some of the magic supply houses or write to suppliers of ventriloquial figures. They will carry vent puppets of all types, mostly animal or crazy character figures made of fur, cloth, or plastic. These are far less expensive than carved or molded figures and are certainly acceptable for ventriloquists. Write to Show-Biz Services (1735 East 26 Street, Brooklyn, New York 11229) for a catalog of vent figures and puppets. We suggest you send one dollar in stamps to cover the cost of postage.

Other Puppet Ideas

Here are some other suggestions for relatively inexpensive puppets.

Sock Puppet: You can make your own puppet from an old cotton or woolen sock. Put your hand all the way into the toe of the sock, your thumb in the heel. If you push a pencil across your thumb so that the material is pushed to the palm of your hand, you will have a more defined line. Stitch the material to either side of the sock, at the crotch of the thumb, and at the end near the base of your little finger. Two buttons sewn on top become its eyes. When using this figure, tip your fingers slightly to make sure the audience always sees the eyes. Both eye and mouth movements are important for the illusion.

Your sock puppet can be used by itself on your arm, or it can stick out of the inside of a bag. Make a hole in the back of the bag to accommodate your hand. Have your puppet pop up from inside (Figure 17). You could do the same thing with a basket, a

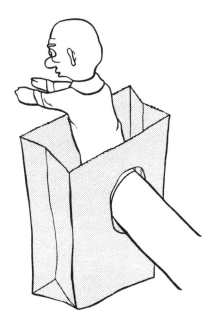

Fig. 17

cereal box, or an overturned hat with a hole in its side. Clowns have puppets coming from inside purses. One ventriloquist uses a small dog puppet that pops out of an airline bag. Use a little imagination and see if you can come up with an idea of your own.

Paper Bag Puppet: A simple puppet can be made from a paper bag. Use a small sandwich bag, size 5 or 6. Lay the bag flat on a table, just the way it is stored at the grocery. You will notice that the bottom is usually folded and creased. Use a crayon or a felt-tip marker to draw teeth, eyes, a nose, and the top and bottom lips. The top lip is on the folded section of the bag; the lower lip is drawn just below the fold. Your hand will go into the bag as in the illustration. Opening and closing your hand will create the mouth action (Figures 18 and 19).

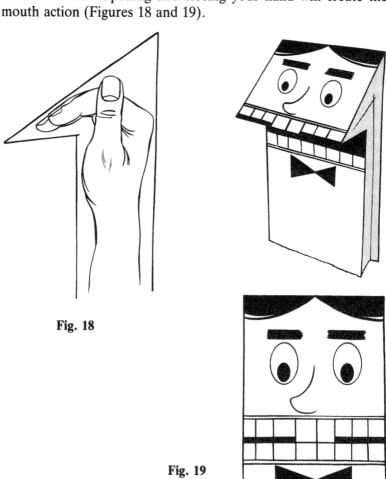

Fig. 18

Fig. 19

Cereal Box Puppet: Use a small cereal box, the type used for single portion servings. Cut the sides of the box exactly in half with a razor. Fold the box back (Figure 20). Cover the outside with colored paper or paint. Use a strong glue to attach two buttons or bottle caps for eyes. Glue these to the upper section. Draw the lips on the upper and lower sections as illustrated (Figure 21). This will work like a standard glove puppet, with four fingers on top and the thumb controlling the lower mouth (Figure 22).

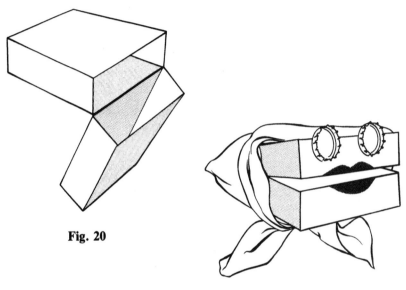

Fig. 20

Fig. 21

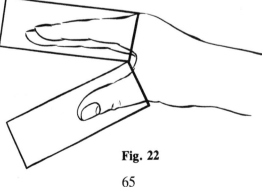

Fig. 22

65

Portable Puppet Theater: Attach a piece of black cloth to a dowel about thirty-six inches long. The cloth should drape nicely in front of your body. The length of the cloth is determined by your height. Attach a false hand to the right side of the dowel so that it looks as if your right hand is holding the dowel. If you can't get a false hand from a magic or joke shop, you can stuff cotton into a few of the fingers from an old white glove and glue these to the cloth. Make sure you have a matching glove on your own left hand. Your real right hand is in the sleeve of your glove puppet. Your left hand holds the dowel in front of you. The illusion is that both of your hands are holding the cloth. Now you can bring the puppet up to the top of the rod so that he can be seen and appears to be talking and acting independently, without any connection to you (Figure 23).

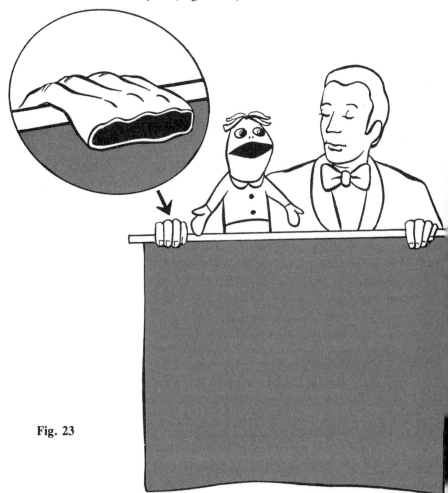

Fig. 23

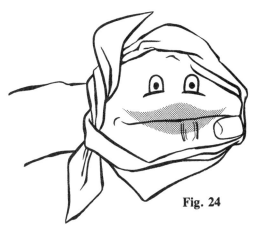

Fig. 24

The Hand Figure: For many years ventriloquists have been doing impromptu shows with the use of hand figures. The artist uses his own hand for the face. To make a hand figure, use grease paint or a deep, dark-colored lipstick to draw the shape of the lips. The color goes around the crotch of the left hand, covering the side of the thumb and the inside of the index finger. Draw the eyes as two circles, one on either side of the knuckles, or draw them as shown in the illustration (Figure 24).

Close the hand into a small fist with the ball of the thumb pressing the side of the index finger at the second joint. Raise and lower the first joint of your thumb to create a mouthlike opening. The ball of the thumb must remain in touch with the index finger. To make the illusion more interesting, wrap a handkerchief around your wrist to resemble a scarf or a gypsy hat. Fold your handkerchief diagonally and tie the two opposite ends in a small knot. Place the handkerchief around your wrist. You may need to use your teeth to pull the knot tighter. One side of the scarf hangs below the face; the other is at the side. Señor Wences popularized this type of figure on television. Instead of a handkerchief, he adds a small wig and body for his character "Johnnie."

Another way to construct a hand figure is to use button eyes instead of painted ones. Attach two small buttons to a piece of strong piano wire. Bend the wire so that it will fit around your hand. One eye is held between the middle and ring fingers at the third joint. The other end of the wire comes over the top of the hand as in the illustrations (Figures 25 and 26). Two painted dots on the index finger resemble nostrils.

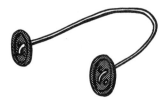

Fig. 25

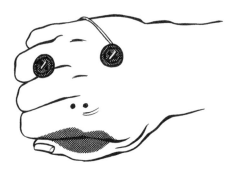

Fig. 26

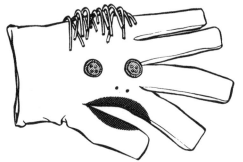

Fig. 27

Fig. 28

The Glove: A portable hand figure can be made from a plain white cotton glove. You can dye or paint the lips on the thumb and index finger as you did for the hand figure. Sew two buttons for the eyes on the back of the glove. Brightly colored fringe or wool can be sewed or glued on for hair (Figure 27).

To make a more realistic figure out of the glove, you can add a small doll's body. Sew a ring on the neck so that you can hold the body under the glove with your little finger. The mouth operates just like the mouth of the hand figure (Figure 28). A few good wrist movements will animate the figure. He can be made to look up or down. Jay Marshall uses a glove character. He adds a pair of long rabbit ears to create "Lefty," the most famous of the glove hand figures.

Jay Marshall and Lefty. Known for his magic work in the better nightclubs of the country, Marshall and his glove have traveled around the world. The public remembers him best for his many appearances on the Ed Sullivan TV show.

7

VENTRILOQUIAL NOVELTIES

Many unusual items can be used in place of a regular figure. Sometimes these are used by professional vents for encores or impromptu performances. Remember that all you need for the illusion is a moving mouth. Here are some of the more popular novelties that have been used in the past. Perhaps you can design one of your own.

Talking Cane: The top of a walking stick is carved with a small head and a trigger to operate the mouth. Numerous kinds of heads are used, either human or animal (birds, snakes, dogs).

Toby Jug: Toby jugs were popular in England years ago, and now the mugs have become collector's items. A face is sculptured on the side of the mug. The mouth control is made from a rubber bulb in the handle of the mug. The cup actually holds liquid, and with a squeeze of the bulb, the mouth can speak to the people in the tavern.

Talking Cork: Some years ago, the small-figure cork was in vogue. This cork had a tiny doll attached and was used to stop an opened wine bottle. A short plunger-type stick was set in the back of the doll. Pressing this stick caused the mouth to move. This allowed a wine bottle to talk. A napkin wrapped around the bottle gave it a costume of sorts.

Talking Skull: A skull was made to speak like a vent figure. The head was usually mounted on a small stand, which contained a trigger to control the spring mouth. In Holland, a man named

Anverdi recently designed a miniature radio-controlled skull that opens and closes its mouth even while the ventriloquist is at least ten feet away.

Head in a Box: Señor Wences, one of the great modern ventriloquists, uses a large face inside a box. The box looks like a large cigar box. When it is opened, it reveals a man with a beard and glasses who promptly says in a husky voice, "Close the door." Wences uses this as a running gag in his act. A variation of this is the Father Time box, which has a clock painted on the front. When the box is opened, a sweet old man in a white beard speaks as Father Time.

Father Time in a box.

Talking Table: Many magicians have used a talking table with a mouth painted on the front drape. A section above is fitted with a spring movement. The mouth is operated from behind the table.

Talking Picture: In this unusual novelty, a photo or a painting in a frame sits on a table or stand. The mouth is rigged so that it can be opened by pulling a lever or wire in the back. Any picture can be rigged for a comedy effect.

Face on a Blackboard: The magician takes a piece of chalk and draws a face on a special blackboard, outlining the gimmick for the mouth. The chalk drawing then speaks to the audience. The mechanism is on the slate but is painted black so that it is unseen by the onlookers.

Frog in a Basket: Use a frog, or any animal puppet, and have him come out of a small fruit basket. Cut a hole in the back of the basket as you did for the sock puppet described in Chapter 6. Any character can come out of the basket. Magicians often use puppet snakes who select cards tossed in the basket.

Chatty Boot: Young Lee Pittsburg cut the bottom of a boot and adapted it to become a talking shoe. The sole drops with the action of his hand, flat on the sole, which works the mouth.

Talking Business Card: Although it is not generally a good idea to perform ventriloquism at too close a range, this impromptu idea will earn you a good reputation. Borrow a business card. Use a pen or a felt-tip marker to draw a pair of eyes, a nose, and part of a mouth on the short end of the unprinted side of the card. Use about one-third of the surface for your drawing.

Bend the card in half with your left hand, but do not crease it. Hold the short end of the card between your left thumb and middle fingers with your index finger separating the ends. Place your right thumb and middle finger at the opposite ends. With your right index finger, press in on the bend to form an indentation. Remove your left hand. By gently squeezing the thumb and middle fingers together, you create a mouth action (Figures 29–31). To dress the character better, you might consider drawing on the opposite printed side to form a lower lip.

When using the business card figure, keep your patter very short and avoid plosive or labial sounds that will give you lip

Fig. 29

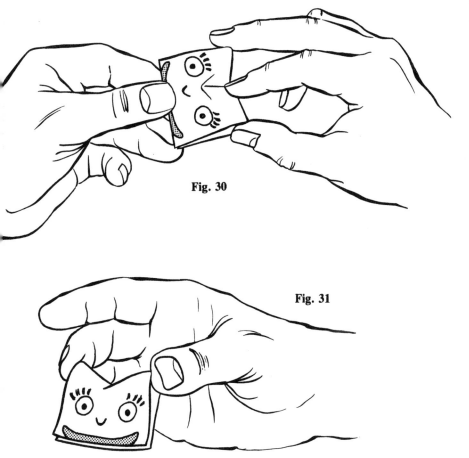

Fig. 30

Fig. 31

The author with Cecil, his talking rabbit. Other puppet friends from left to right: a People Puppet; Frog in a Basket; People puppet; Stanley, a vent figure; puppet Crow, Handsome Harry, a vent figure; and a Pelham Girl puppet. (Stanley was molded by Alan Szemok. Harry is an Olson figure.)

Howard Olson and Dancin' Sam. Sam can dance and sing at the same time.

Paul Stadelman demonstrates a talking Bear.

movement problems. "Yes" and "no" answers to your questions will do nicely. "So long" is preferred to "goodbye."

The most unusual vent novelty I have seen is a two-headed vent figure mounted on a single control stick. The figure was made by John Carroll and was used by Roy Douglas. Both of these men are dead, but the figure lives on, displayed at the Flosso-Hornmann Magic Shop on West 34th Street in Manhattan. The glass cases in the shop are part of a small museum that also has the Punch and Judy figures belonging to Harry Houdini and a few rare old vent figures such as a miniature head and an extremely old black Madame Pinxy figure.

The world's largest collection of novelties and rare vent figures is in the Vent Haven Museum in Fort Mitchell, Kentucky.

8

THE DISTANT VOICE

By now you probably are fairly proficient with the "near" ventriloquist voice and have acquired an acceptable second voice. You are able to pronounce all the difficult sounds, and your animation and figure handling is on its way to perfection. If this is not the case, read this chapter anyway, but do not try to achieve the "distant" sounds until later in your vent development.

The distant voice is one that seems to come from a place far away from the ventriloquist. While the voice is not actually "thrown" anywhere, the illusion makes the spectator believe it comes from afar.

The development of the "distant" voice will take some training. You need a great deal of practice and a bit of patience with yourself.

Creating the illusion of distance also requires some knowledge of audience psychology. A voice coming from far away will be faint but clear enough for people to understand what is being said. It is generally a quiet voice but with a higher pitch than you would use in normal conversation. Think of trying to talk to someone on the other side of a lake. If you shouted "hello" from your side, your listener would hear only the sounds "eh" and "oh." At a distance, consonants cannot be heard. "Hello" would sound like "eh-oh." If you were closer, perhaps halfway across the lake, he might hear "ello."

The distant voice is forced from your throat and has a strained quality. To create the thin voice required for distant ventriloquism you must be able to control the way your sounds are made. To get the proper control you will need to learn the *drone* or *buzz* sound, which will develop your skill in hitting it correctly each time.

First say a simple "ah." Your lips should be parted, with the tip of your tongue touching the top of your teeth just at the gum line. Your tongue must be arched upward a bit. Tighten up on your stomach muscles. Open your throat as though you were about to yawn. Get a good breath of air. Now let the air escape as you sound the "ah." Draw out the sound as though you were imitating the drone of an airplane. Tighten your stomach muscles a little more to get the sound deeper in your throat. Relax. Now pretend that you are trying to pick up a very heavy package and, as you do so, grunt. Think about where the sound is coming from. It might sound as though it were down inside your stomach. Try not to strain your voice too much in making these sounds.

Use the same technique to produce a humming "mm" sound. This "mm" sound should be practiced so that you can imitate the buzzing of a small fly around your head. Make it louder to sound like a bumble bee. You will know the correct sound when you hit it; it will be clear and without too much strain. You will be forcing the air through tensed vocal cords, and this pressure will create the sound.

Do not practice this for long periods of time or you will strain your vocal cords. Practice the drone or buzz tone, each time holding the sound longer. First do a drone for ten seconds, then fifteen seconds, and so on. After a few days try to vary the sound by changing its intensity. Make it sound farther away or closer. You will do this by raising or lowering the pitch. To develop different sounds try a few variations:

ah . . . oh . . . ee

Try Howard Olson's "Catching a Fly" exercise.

Catching a Fly: Hold a small drinking glass in one hand with its mouth up. Pretend there is a fly buzzing around your head and create a gentle buzz sound. Turn your head to follow it and allow it to stop as you look after it. The sound must get louder as the fly gets closer to you. Pretend to see it coming closer and start the tone again. Move your head up and down or back and forth a little as though you were watching the fly flitting around. This is all part of the illusion and here you must remember to be an actor. Pretend to scoop up the fly with the glass. Continue the buzzing sound. Bring the other hand over quickly and cover the mouth of the glass as though you caught the fly. When the fly has been caught, change the pitch of the buzz by arching your tongue upward to cut off the flow of air. The sound goes further back in the throat, and the fly seems to be inside the glass. Remove the hand covering the glass as you bring the sound back to the original buzz. Pretend the fly has flown away. The intensity of the sound fades to nothing.

Vocal magic is created with the voice box, but you, the voice magician, have to help it along with more misdirection. A figure or puppet on your knee will provide the misdirection needed for "near" vent, but when the voice comes from afar, you will need the spectator's eye, as well as his ear. If you look up, your spectator also will look up. If a voice is supposed to be coming from the ceiling, you should be looking up there. When a voice comes from below, look down. But before you can convince the listener, you should "set him up" by *conditioning* him. You must set the stage so that the listener expects to hear the sound coming from its proper place *before* you have created that sound. Here are some examples.

Traveling Sound: Paul Stadelman used a demonstration in which he first explained what was going to happen and then allowed it to happen. First he prepared his listeners. He used a paper cone. "I have a sound trapped in the bottom of this cone," he said. His hand covered the opening. "If I hold the mouth of this cone upward, the sound will come out and go toward the ceiling. If I turn it over, the sound will travel down. Let me show you. Please listen." Now the spectators were ready to hear what Stadelman wanted them to hear.

Hold the cone so that the opening faces your other hand. Start your drone, "eee." Tilt the cone mouth up toward the ceiling and make the sound a bit louder *as you look up toward the ceiling*. Add some pressure so that the sound will be of a higher intensity than normal. Now turn the cone and *look down* as you lower the intensity, bringing the drone to a lower pitch. Your eyes must follow the action.

Voice in a Bottle: I had lunch in London one afternoon with Terri Rogers. We were talking about show business, as performers often do. The subject of distant voices came up and Terri proceeded with her favorite demonstration. She called the waiter over to the table. "Waiter, I think there is something wrong with my wine."

The waiter was upset and asked, "What seems to be wrong?"

Terri pointed to the corked bottle on the table. "Please come closer and listen." She lifted the cork slightly and then put it back quickly. "Did you hear that?"

Of course, the waiter heard nothing. "No, madam."

"I heard it. Listen please," said Terri, as she removed the cork again. This time the waiter was straining to hear the sound, and it came. Terri, in a perfect distant voice from the bottle, said, "Let me out."

The waiter was perplexed. He heard a sound. It sounded like a tiny voice deep inside the bottle, shouting to get out. He looked almost frightened, then suddenly realized that something strange was going on. Finally he smiled and said, "Please do that again. I want the manager to listen."

The psychology Terri used to set up the waiter was perfect. He didn't hear the sound the first time. But he was convinced beforehand that there was going to be a sound. He listened harder. And since his ear and his mind were trained on the bottle, the sounds seemed to come from inside rather than from Terri.

Come on Down: Try this exercise. Pretend that you are going to speak with someone on the roof, or up the stairs. First rehearse "a-e-i-o-u" in a drone or distant voice. Then practice reciting the numbers one through ten. As you say each number make your voice a trifle louder. Try not to strain. Look up at the ceiling, cup your hand near your mouth, and almost shout. "Are you coming down?"

"Yes." *(A barely audible "distant" voice)*
"Count the steps on the way down." *(Normal voice)*
"One, two, three," *("Distant" voice, but more audible)*
"Four, five, six," *(Slightly louder, lower in pitch)*

"Seven, eight, nine," *(Clear and much louder)*
"Ten. Here I am." *(Regular vent voice)*

Australian ventriloquist Clifford Guest uses a distant voice to imitate the sounds of a foxhunt. You hear the hoofbeats of the horses as they get closer, then you hear faraway voices shouting, "Tally-ho." Then you hear barking dogs and finally the hoofbeats again as they fade into the distance.

9

THE MUFFLED VOICE

The muffled voice is in between the "near" and "distant" voices. It is sometimes referred to as the "near-distant" voice. It combines both techniques. The sound generally comes from a place nearby, but it is not a clear, loud sound. It is used for the classic "Figure in a Suitcase Bit," in which the sound apparently comes from inside a closed suitcase. The same voice would be heard from behind a closed door, or when you have a heavy muffler around your neck in the winter and try to speak through it. The voice is made by throttling the sound coming from your throat. The air supply is cut off as the tongue gets in the way of a clear sound. To see how the method works, try this with a cigar box. You should have a good, working near vent voice when you do this. Open the box and look inside before you start to speak.

>   V: What are you doing in there?
>   F: Nothing. Close the lid; there's a draft in here.
>   V: If I snap it shut, how will you breathe?
>   F: On second thought, I'll come out.
>   V: Never mind. I'll close the lid. *(Start to do so)*

At this point, take in a good breath of air, make the vent voice louder as you have him say:

>   F: No, no, don't close it.

As you close the lid halfway, arch your tongue to throttle the sound. Tighten your stomach muscles as though you were

81

holding the distant voice. Lower the lid of the box, snapping it shut.

> F: Let me out of here! Let me out!

When you have it right, the muffled sound will appear to come from inside the box.

When you use a distant voice, remember that the voice should come from a logical place. The illusion is better if the voice is coming from a place where a person might be, rather than from inside a bottle. Try this. Walk to a closet door and knock on it.

> V: Are you in there? *(No sound; open the closet door)*
> F: What do you want? *(Regular vent voice)*
> V: Excuse me. I'm looking for George.
> F: I'll see if he's here. George!
> Distant voice: What do you want?
> F: Someone is here looking for you.
> Distant voice: Tell him go away.
> F: He said to go away.
> V: Thanks a lot! *(Close the door)*
> Muffled voice: And don't come back.

This is a scene with four voices. It uses some acting to produce the illusion. The closet is a logical place for the voice to be. The misdirection of opening the door and looking inside will help, but try to remember to control your lip movement for each of the voices.

10

THE TELEPHONE VOICE

If you have a tape recorder, set it on a table near your phone, call a friend, and, with his permission, record the conversation. Make sure the recorder picks up the voice from a distance of a foot or more from the receiver. The sound you hear is almost a distant voice. Try to imitate this sound using distant voice techniques. You can get a prop phone, called a Phoney Ring Telephone, at most novelty or magic shops. The ringing device fits in your pocket, and when you push the button, it produces a sound like a real telephone. The earpiece is in your pocket or is attached to your coat with a safety pin. Pull the phone out and answer it. Your audience will hear the sound apparently coming from the phone. *Look at the receiver* when you are supposed to be listening. Pull it away from your ear so everyone can listen.

> Voice: Hello. Is that you, George?
> V: Yes, this is George.
> Voice: Are you sure it's George?
> V: It's me all right. George.
> Voice: George, can you lend me five dollars?
> V: I'll tell him when he comes in. *(Hang up)*

If you can master the phone voice you can have a three-way conversation with the voice on the phone and your figure. Here is a sample phone dialogue.

A Phone Routine

(Your prop phone rings from a small table near you, or from your pocket.)

F: If that's the telephone, tell them I'm not here.
V: Hello . . . hello.
Voice: Hello . . . hello.
F: Must be talking to an echo.
Voice: Hello. Is this two, oh, oh, oh? (2, 0, 0, 0)
V: Did you want two, oh, oh, oh?
F: Ho, ho to you too.
Voice: Two, zero, zero, zero.
F: That's a lot of nothing.
V: This is two, zero, zero, zero. Who did you want to speak to?
Voice: Is that you?
F: Is there someone in that thing? *(Looks into receiver)*
V: This is me.
Voice: Can I speak to *(name of your figure)?*
V: He wants to speak to you.
F: Tell him I'm out.

The next three lines are done rapidly, changing voices.

Voice: Is he there?
V: He's here.
F: I'm here.
V: Okay, speak to him.
F: I'm scared.
V: Go ahead and talk to him.
F: I don't think I want to do it. *(Louder)* I won't do it.
V: Now be quiet and say something.
F: *(moves mouth, no sound).*
V: What are you doing?
F: I'm being quiet and saying something.
Voice: Is this two, oh, oh, oh?
F: Oh, oh. *(Into phone)* Yes, who is this?
Voice: Hello, hello.
F: What do you want?
Voice: Can you lend me twenty dollars?

84

F: I can't hear you.

Voice: Can you lend me twenty dollars?

F: I said I can't hear you.

V: I can hear him.

F: Then *you* lend him the twenty.

Voice: *(says something unintelligible)*.

F: You don't say! *(More voice sounds)* You don't say!
(Voice sound again a bit faster) You don't say! Goodbye.
(Hangs up)

V: What was that all about?

F: He didn't say.

11

TRICKS OF THE TRADE

Long scripts cannot keep the audience's attention if they become tedious. The average vent act of about fifteen minutes needs more than just a comedy exchange and a song. You can introduce several characters to break up the act. You can also do some interesting stunts and demonstrations with your distant or phone voice. Here are some bits and tricks that you may be able to add to or adapt for your performance.

Drinking: It is technically impossible to drink while you are talking or singing. The audience isn't aware of this. The average person believes that it can be done by someone with special talent. There are several ways to accomplish the illusion of drinking while the figure sings or hums. First, you can use a trick glass like those used by magicians. The Mod Glass or the Vanishing Milk Glass are the names of two trick products that simulate full glasses of liquid. Milk or a dark-colored soda is needed. The glasses are constructed so that only a small amount of liquid is used to make the glass itself look full. I won't describe the mechanics, since they are magicians' secrets, but the glasses can be purchased at magic shops. The illusion is that a full glass of milk is tipped to your lips. No liquid actually comes out, but when the glass is turned upright, only half or a third of the liquid remains. These glasses cost less than ten dollars.

No trick can substitute for the real thing, however. Once you can sustain a note in the vent voice, you can practice with a real glass of liquid. You should use a thick-walled shot glass. The glass in the illustration (Figure 32) is enlarged to show you the

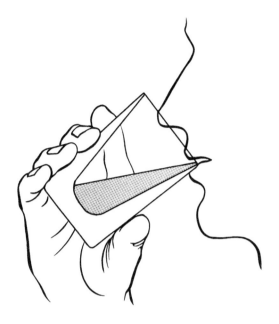

Fig. 32

detail of the type of glass to use. The glass actually holds a small amount of liquid. Ask a bartender to recommend a glass that will hold less than an ounce. Use a dark liquid such as grape soda. Make sure it is *not carbonated.* Pick up your glass at the end of a song, holding the figure's last note. Drink by allowing the liquid to pour into your mouth, around the tongue. Show the glass empty, finish the note and bow, along with your figure. Swallow the liquid as you bow. It will take a great deal of practice and some choking, but don't give up. If you can master it, it is a very convincing vent trick.

Smoking: Smoking is not recommended for any ventriloquist. Aside from the fact that it can greatly impair your health, it definitely restricts your breathing and the clear production of sound. Years ago, a figure was often equipped with a bulb at the end of a long tube that went through the head and was attached to the mouth. The figure was given a cigarette, and by squeezing the tube the vent could make it appear to be smoking. For the vent to smoke while the figure hums, he must blow through the cigarette, causing the end to glow and giving the appearance that he is actually puffing on it. Be prepared to cough a lot.

Blowing out the Match: Here is an idea that may earn you extra bookings. Write a script about the dangers of smoking. The figure will tell you how bad it can be. Every time you try to light a cigarette, the figure can blow out the match. Here is how to do it.

With a cigarette in your mouth, hold a lighted match about six inches below it and to the side. You can blow downward, pulling your lower lip back slightly. As you blow it out, the figure will lean forward toward the match. The illusion is that *he* blew it out. If you use a wooden match, you can hold it about an eighth of an inch above its bottom, between your thumb and index finger. Using the fingernail of the middle finger, snap the bottom of the wood. This will cause the match to go out. The figure, of course, must lean toward the match at the same time.

To light the match, you could glue a small piece of striking surface to the side of the figure's ear. Striking the match this way provides extra comedy. You could also wrap the head of the match in some of the striking paper from a book of matches. A strong rubber band will hold it in place. Pin the striking paper under your coat so that when you reach for the match, it strikes the paper on the way out of your coat. This may be dangerous, so be very careful in the handling. Magic shops sell a device that will do this.

You can have some fun with a relighting candle sold in many party shops. This is a small candle that cannot be blown out. Have the figure blow it out, and after a second or two it will relight.

Blowing Bubbles: This bit uses the same principle as the match gag. Buy a bottle of dime store bubbles. (They come with a small plastic wand that has an open circle on top.) Dip the circle into the liquid and lightly blow the top to produce bubbles. To increase the number of bubbles, add a few drops of liquid detergent to the bubble liquid. Make sure that you work near a table. Keep a towel handy to wipe spills.

The bubbles are made by blowing a steady stream of air through your parted lips, as with the match bit. After the figure has blown the bubbles two or three times, he announces, "Once more, the hard way." (Turn his head to the rear and have a few bubbles blown.) This is a great stunt for children's parties and school shows. Practice this several times to get the correct angle at which to hold the plastic wand.

Whistling: Here is a gag idea. Your figure begins to whistle as you drink a glass of water. The whistle is done offstage by someone else as you go through the motions. After the applause, repeat the trick. This time, drink, take a bow, and let the whistling continue. Wave to someone offstage until the whistling stops. The audience will catch on, and after the laugh, have the figure ask, "How else, folks?" If you are one of those lucky people who can whistle through your teeth, *you* can whistle for your partner.

The Harmonica Bit: You will need two harmonicas for this gag. Pick up a cheap one-inch harmonica and a regular six-inch one. The little one should be made of metal and should actually play. You should be able to practice a simple tune like "Oh Susannah" on the little one without having to hold it. It must be played while you hold it between your lips. Paint the bottom of the small harmonica with acrylic paint. Try to find a color close to your own lip color. Attach the small harmonica to the big one with a small square of beeswax or magician's wax (Figure 33). Have the two harmonicas in your pocket or on a table nearby. When you are ready, offer the harmonica to the figure.

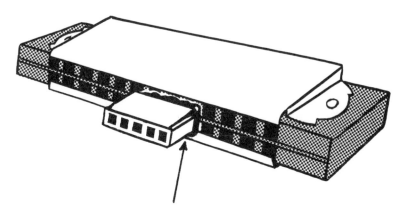

Fig. 33 Small harmonica attached with wax.

> V: Can you play this?
> F: Sure.
> V: Let me see if it works.

Put the small harmonica between your lips and blow through it. Then dislodge the wax, keeping the small one in your mouth. Place the large one at your figure's mouth.

If you turn your head toward the figure and lift your arm slightly as you play, the little harmonica will not be visible to the audience. When the song is finished, remove the large one from his lips and blow the last note. You are really attaching the two together again. Both go into your pocket as you take your bow.

A small box can be built under the seat of your figure to store small props such as a telephone, a glass of liquid. or a harmonica. A small cassette player can also be hidden there for special effects.

All by Himself: The figure's mouth can be operated with your foot if you need both hands to play an instrument or do magic tricks. Attach the trigger to the top end of a bass drum pedal (without the drum beater). The mechanism can be hidden behind the chair in which the figure will be seated. Stepping on the pedal will activate the mouth. This will allow freedom for both your hands. Do not use this arrangement too often, however, or you will lose valuable animation.

Something in His Eye: You will use a pocket handkerchief for this bit. The figure complains and you try to get a cinder from his eye by wiping it with the cloth.

> F: I got something in my eye.
> V: I'll get it out. Sit still.
> F: What are you doing?
> V: Sit still.
> F: You're putting more in than you're taking out!

Squirt Flower: Your figure can wear a novelty squirting flower, which you can get in most joke or magic novelty shops. The flower is in his lapel; the tube goes under his coat and rests alongside the headstick. Squeeze the bulb and the flower will squirt water. The following radio bit can be used with the flower.

You will need a small box, about the size of a pack of cigarettes. Cover it with construction paper and draw a dial on the face so that it resembles a transistor radio. Do not use a real radio. It must look fake.

> V: Here's my radio. Let me get the weather report.
> F: That's a radio?
> V: Yes it is. Let me tune it in. *(Use a "distant" voice for static, varying it with singing and talking as you pretend to turn the dial.)*

Radio: The weather is clear.

> F: It's going to rain.

Radio: No. I said it was clear.

> F: It's going to rain.
> V: How do you know it's going to rain?
> F: I just know. *(Turn the figure toward you and squeeze the bulb to squirt the water at your own face.)*

Another Phone Bit: If you use a gag telephone you can do many cute bits. The Great Lester used to speak to Heaven on the phone. He would ask for someone and the telephone voice would be heard calling to an even more distant voice. Modern vent Dan Ritchard speaks on the phone to someone who does a tap dance. Not only do you hear the taps, but Dan also hums along to provide the music. Here is a cute bit to include in the act.

> *(Phone rings: vent answers.)*
> V: Hello. Oh it's you.
> Voice: Do you love me?
> V: You know that I love you.
> Voice: Say that you love me.
> V: Okay. I love you.
> Voice *(says something unintelligible).*
> V: Yes, he's here. I'll tell him.

As you put the phone away, lean over to any man in the audience and say, "That was your wife. She said she'll be home late."

Head Turn:

> F: Are you sure there's nothing behind me?
> V: Nothing.

After you speak, the figure rotates his head 360 degrees. The head spin is a very cute stunt that will get laughs for you.

12

PUTTING YOUR ACT TOGETHER

Once you have mastered the vocal and animation techniques that bring your figure to life, you are ready to start thinking about your act. How will you present the complete package? What will you say and do?

You know that your lips will not move; your voice is different from that of the figure; and he has his own personality. Now you must tell this to the audience.

The elements of your act will be combined into a smooth, flowing sequence called a *routine*. You will need a script that tells you which lines you will say and which lines are for the figure. You must decide how to play the act. Will you be standing or sitting in front of the audience? You must choose your music, a good introduction, and a short encore. You will learn how to take a bow and be gracious. You will learn how to use a microphone. You will have a plan for getting on and off the stage without tripping on the wires. You will learn that showmanship and presentation are very important aspects of becoming an entertainer. In the pages that follow, I will try to put these elements into perspective for you.

Give your partner a name—one that is easy to pronounce and cute enough to be remembered by the audience. If he is a regular kid, pick a common name; if he is an odd character, choose a very odd one. Paul Stadelman's figure was called Windy Higgins. The name was copyrighted and, in fact, was listed in the Chicago phone book while Paul was alive. Windy was a great name for a talker. Many people remember the names of the figures and sometimes forget the ventriloquist. Charlie McCarthy, Jerry Mahoney, Danny O'Day, and Mortimer Snerd were famous names in recent history. See if you can remember who their partners were.*

Your partner now has a name and a costume, either similar or in sharp contrast to yours. Make sure your clothing is properly tailored so you both look your very best. Keep your clothing clean and pressed at all times. Charlie McCarthy was patterned after a Chicago newsboy. In his early days he wore a sweater and a cap. Years later, Edgar Bergen gave him a more sophisticated image and the costume became a top hat and tuxedo. Charlie's voice and character fit his personality and dress.

Think about how your little friend will act, think, and talk. You know what his voice sounds like. If he has a gruff voice, he probably won't be a cherubic or a pixielike character. Talk to your friend as you rehearse and get to know him. Make up your mind what his likes and dislikes are.

Selecting Material

Once you have decided on the personality of the character you have created, you will be able to select the material needed for the act. If your little partner is a wise-cracking, cheeky boy, he will be given all the smart-aleck lines and you must be the straight man. The act need not be all gags, but can build with jokes coming from the situations you create. If you are in a sketch, the props and scenery help develop the script. If you do a stand-up act—just you and the figure with no props or scenery— you are restricted to an exchange of lines like those in the scripts prepared at the end of this book. If you can sing, you should find easy song material suitable to the theme of your act. Perhaps you could add a song parody for more comedy.

Your act needs an opening, a good middle section, and a strong closing. In the beginning, the audience will evaluate you and your technique before accepting the act. Your opening,

*Edgar Bergen, Paul Winchell, Jimmy Nelson, Edgar Bergen.

therefore, should be easy to perform, with a minimum of difficult sounds. You should start with funny material and establish your character as soon as possible. It is in the first few minutes that the audience looks for lip movement. Once the illusion is created, they will forget you are a ventriloquist and will accept the two of you as a comedy team.

I suggest that your emcee not use the title "ventriloquist" when he introduces you. He can refer to you and your partner by name, or announce a comedy team. Your audience will see that you are a vent when you enter, but why alert them to your technique rather than to the entertainment you are going to provide? Remember the key word—entertainment. Give it to them.

Set the theme of your act as soon as possible. Plan your material for the opening. Figure out how you intend to hold the figure—on your lap, on a chair, on a stand. If you are going to use a chair, make sure you know how it will get to the center of the stage before you arrive, or plan to take it with you when you enter. Arrange to have your microphone set at the proper level between the two of you. The figure should be animated when you both arrive at center stage. Perhaps he can talk to you. Have him turn his head to look at the crowd or the orchestra. Then begin, confidently, with your opening line:

V: Isn't it great to be working here tonight?
F: With our act, it's great to be working anywhere!

You're off to a good start.

Choose the theme of your act according to the type of audience you have. If you play to a family crowd the lines should be funny to adults as well as to children. Limit yourself to topics with which everyone is familiar. Talk about the weather, pollution, health, diet, television shows, cars, traffic, marriage, occupations, restaurants, prices, and so on. If you have a schoolboy or schoolgirl character, you could talk about school subjects such as arithmetic, spelling, teachers, grades, sports, and the like.

When working for children, remember that the little ones, ages four through seven, do not understand gags and jokes. To them, your partner is a talking doll. They will enjoy just plain conversation or perhaps poems and nursery rhymes. Older children, ages eight through eleven, will accept the figure as one of their own kind. From twelve to sixteen, youngsters must be treated as young adults and given material to match their intelligence. Never play down to a child. Children understand and sense a performer's attitude toward them very quickly.

The middle or body of your act should be sprinkled with comedy and must further develop the theme you have chosen. Once you have created the illusion, and the audience has accepted your doll as real, you can dress the act with a few tricks such as muffled voices and distant lines and perhaps a phone bit. You can also introduce other figures and characters, but make sure the transition from one to another is smooth.

Your closing should be strong, with powerful gag lines or a final punch line to the act. You could also close with music or a song parody. Make sure you can sing in tune if you decide to use a song ending. A few singing lessons might help. Many vents close with the "Suitcase Bit." The figure is put back into his suitcase and frantically tries to escape. Move the head and feet from side to side, pretending that he jumps out each time. Finally you close the case and walk off with the muffled voice yelling, "Let me out."

Be sure to return to the stage with the figure for a curtain call. Youngsters must be able to see that he is all right. You must have a happy, living figure at the close of your act. Have an encore prepared and use it before your final bow.

Writing Your Own Material

Selecting the right comedy material is the most difficult part of your business. The singer is aided by a vast store of music to fit his style and vocal capability. The actor is given a script, designed for the character he is to play. But unfortunately the comedian, disc jockey, ventriloquist, and emcee must be original and unique. The most upsetting thing the entertainer can hear is the hushed phrase, "That's an old one."

There is nothing wrong with an old joke for someone who hasn't heard it before. But why take chances? You can make your material fresh and sparkling, to fit your individual image, style, and delivery. The best thing to do, of course, is to hire a professional gag writer or an act doctor who can do this for you. He is the tailor who can mold material to fit the performer perfectly. However, the entertainer who is new to the business cannot affort the luxury of a full-time writer. If you can't buy free-lance material, the next best thing is to borrow, steal, switch, and write your own gags.

First of all, start a gag file of your own. Clip and save every joke you read. Jot down every good gag you hear and every idea that pops into your head. A library will have a good many books written by top-notch jokesters. You can find joke books, comedy records, and quotes in your newspaper columns, all within easy reach. There are several good comedy services, which can supply "stock" collections of special types of material. Collect and read all the gags you can. It might get to the point where the gags won't seem funny anymore. Don't give up hope. Good material often does not "read" funny on paper.

If you seriously want to put your own material together, you should be aware of the basic formulas used in comedy writing. Once you become familiar with these principles you will find it easier to switch material and make existing material more comfortable for your type of performance. You will also begin to "think funny" and write your own lines. You'll know when and where and how to work them into usable routines.

The following examples will give you an idea of each basic formula so you will be able to recognize each style. The examples are not all ventriloquist gags. I will show you how to convert them to your own needs later.

Understatement: The punch line underplays the reality of the situation.

> I was just thrown out of the bar. The guy kicked me,
>   punched me in the eye, and knocked out my tooth.
> That's awful!
> Sure is. I got the feeling he didn't like me!

Exaggeration: The punch line magnifies the truth and blows it out of proportion.

> He's such a terrible sinner.
> Why doesn't he phone "Dial a Prayer"?
> He did! They hung up on him.

My girl has bony knees.
Lots of girls have bony knees.
Up to the shoulders?

False Logic:

Sam, while they go to the moon, we'll go to the sun.
Max, we'll burn up.
Sh . . . we'll go at night.

I drink peanut milk.
How do you get milk from a peanut?
I use a very low stool.

You have a wristwatch in your stomach.
I know, Doc. I swallowed it when I was a kid.
Has it given you trouble before?
Only when I wind it.

Misuse of Words:

I was so surprised when I heard the scream, I couldn't believe my eyes.

One night he went to sleep perfectly healthy; next morning he woke up; he was dead.

I am not always right, but I am never wrong. (Sam Goldwyn)

She has beautiful hands. I'm having a bust made of them.

Puns: A pun is a play on words that sound like other words. Homonyms, words that sound the same but have different meanings, make great puns.

I took my girl to Italy.
Genoa?
No, I just met her.

Drink up. Skoal!
It should be. There's ice in it.

97

He's a baker. He makes lots of dough.
Well, he kneads it.
Boy, you have a lot of crust to tell a crummy joke like that.

Man comes from monkeys.
Not Welshmen.
How come?
They come from Wales.

One Iranian phones another Iranian.
Oh, a Persian to Persian phone call.

Insults:

If I were your wife I'd poison the coffee.
If I were your husband I'd drink it.

Is that perfume I smell?
It is and you do.

I heard a lot about your singing.
Oh, it's nothing.
Yes, that's what I heard.

Reversal:

You know what a race track is.
That's where windows clean people.

My frog is sick.
What's wrong with him?
He's got a man in his throat.

Reversing Obvious Conclusions:

Law is funny. They lock up the jury and let the prisoner out on bail.

The baby stork asked, "Mama, where do I come from?"

Non sequiturs: The conclusion does not follow from the premise.

My stocks went from 4¼ up to 6 back to 5¼ and then 7 . . . and in case of fire dial 711.

My dear man, you have a severe psychosis, complicated by a
   small neurosis, and blended with manic tendencies.
So tell me, Doc, how's the family?

The water here is not too great. We filter it, then boil it, and
   add chemicals.
And then it's good enough to drink?
No . . . we order beer.

Sarcasm: Mild insults.

How much are your apples?
Two cents each, lady.
I'll take one
Are you givin' a party?

The flies in this hotel are thick.
What did you expect for five bucks a day? Flies with a
   college degree?

Was I driving too fast, officer?
No. You were flying too low.

Repetition: Running gags.

I was hunting and shot a bear in the yours. . . .
What's a yours?
Scotch and soda, what's a yours?

(Later in the act)

We traveled until we came to the hidden shores.
What shores?
Scotch and soda, what's yours?

Another type of repetition occurs when the key word in the
buildup appears in the punch line.

Doc, why do I get dizzy when I look down from a tall
   building?
Easy. Your optic nerve presses on the oblongata, which
   sends a signal to the brain endings. Any questions?
Yes. Why do I get dizzy when I look down from a tall
   building?

Toppers:

You're not smart enough to talk to an idiot.
Okay, I'll send you a letter.

You're one step away from an imbecile.
So, I'll move away from you.

Now a song that's sweeping the country.
That's what you should be doing.
Singing?
No, sweeping.

These examples should familiarize you with some of the formula gags used in writing comedy material. A single comedy line is called a *one-liner.* Comedians may put together a string of one-liners to form a monologue. The ventriloquist needs two-line gags to be spoken by two people. One is a set-up line; the second is the punch line. These are called *double gags.*

The thinking process that you should follow when trying to write comedy lines is very logical. First you should pick the subject of your gag. Let's assume the topic is driving. Write down all the words and ideas that come to mind on the subject. You will need gags on cars, traffic, policemen, traffic signals, taxis. Decide on the location or scene of your joke. Where did this all take place? On the road? In your garage? Now, free associate with these ideas. Your gag files will help you pick out gags on the subject, but also think of your own situations, things that could happen while you are driving, who you see, what other cars and people are doing. Now write them all down in a rough sketch. Here are some ideas taken from my own gag files.

My father drove a horse and buggy. Father drove the horse and Mother drove him buggy.

I like to drive. You run across such interesting people.

I have a new car. I just learned to aim it.

It's a five-passenger car. One drives and four people push.

He got a ticket for double parking. His car was on top of another one.

Now you have some gags. The subject is established, and you need a routine. Put a group of gags together into logical sequence. But these are one-liners. You need double gags. So convert them. Break the line into two parts, the buildup and the punch line. Give the figure the punch line.

V: What do you know about driving?
F: My father drove a horse and buggy.
V: I didn't know that.
F: Father drove the horse and Mother drove him buggy.

V: I heard you have a new car.
F: Yes, and I just learned how to aim it.
V: What kind of car is that?
F: A five-passenger car.
V: That's pretty big.
F: One guy drives and four guys push.
V: That's silly.
F: Sure is. I got a ticket for double parking.
V: Where did you park?
F: On top of another car.

Put enough lines together on the same topic and you have a script. Notice the way the set-up lines helped develop the punch lines (the funny ones).

You can change comedy lines to fit your own theme by merely changing the names and places and keeping the framework of the joke. Here is an example of how this is done.

I took your underwear to the laundry.
Great. Where is it now?
They refused it.

We need car and driving lines, so we change the gag:

I sent your car to the car wash.
Great. What happened?
They refused it.

In a famous cartoon, the stewardess is talking to a noisy child in the airplane. She says, "Why don't you go play outside?" Here is how we might switch that for our routine.

F: That pesty neighbor's kid was all over my car.
V: How did you get rid of him?
F: I told him to go out and play in the traffic.

Regular jokes are funnier when you localize them. Add a few names and places that are familiar to the audience and the material sounds as though your story lines were true instead of being jokes. Here is an old joke.

A policeman stopped a drunk on a one-way street and asked, "Where are you going?" "I don't know," the drunk answered, "but I must be late, because everyone else is coming back."

Make it local, name the drunk, name the street, and put yourself and your partner in the picture. It might sound like this.

F: I was late. I'm sorry.
V: What happened?
F: A policeman stopped *(name of local person)*.
V: What for?
F: Well, he had a few drinks and was driving uptown on Market Street.
V: Market Street is a one-way downtown.
F: Well, the cop asked him where he was going.
V: What did *(name of local man)* say?
F: He said, "I don't know, but I must be late because everyone else is coming back."

Remember that you must choose material that will fit you or your character. A small boy character wouldn't tell jokes about his wife. If you tell a story make it plausible. Don't do jokes that are not comfortable for you. Stay away from ethnic or dialect jokes. Try to draw pictures with your stories or jokes.

How cold is it out there?
The icicles on my car are wearing earmuffs.

Don't rush with the punch lines. Allow the audience a moment to get the picture, then hit them with the topper line. Put all your joke lines into a nice sequence and write yourself a script. Edit it, and try to change words that are difficult to pronounce. If you don't have to use *p, b,* or *m* words, why make it hard for yourself?

Now you are ready to pull everything together into an act.

Routining and Timing

Your routine is the presentation of your material in a fixed sequence that you have prepared in advance. You have collected and written the jokes you want to use and selected the song, if any, that you want to sing in the act. Everything must be put together in a special order that you will follow every time you perform your act. The sequence must be interesting from beginning to end. This sequence *is* your act. As I mentioned earlier, the act has three parts—an opening, a middle, and a closing. The opening will get the audience interested in you as soon as possible. The middle will sustain the interest, and the closing will wow them.

Once they have accepted your figure as real, they will be listening to the material and enjoying the fun. Some gag lines will get laughs and others will not. You must experiment. Test the gags and bits by using them in different sequences under different conditions for various audiences. Perhaps you did not get laughs because the delivery was bad. Your delivery, the way you say your lines, can be changed by speaking them slower or faster or by changing the wording.

It is important that the audience understand every word of your dialogue. Make sure the lines are clearly spoken. Test all the jokes and bits, and if you can tape record audience reactions you will hear the places where you always get laughs. Keep those lines, and discard the weaker gags. Many gags do not read well on paper and yet are very funny. By the same token, some hilarious gags that you love do not play well. You must be a fair judge of your audience reaction. The act must move along on an upward swing.

Timing is very important in comedy of any kind. You must learn how and when to deliver every line. Never be in a hurry to get to the next line of the script if you see that the last line is still getting a reaction. Wait for every laugh before you speak again.

Never talk over a laugh line. React to the laughs. If your figure says something that everyone else laughs at, smile and chuckle at it yourself. If the gag doesn't get the laugh it should, do not wait; go directly to the next line. A pause in the wrong place can be deadly. Pace your material so that the speed of your delivery is based on the audience reaction.

Sometimes a good laugh line will not get the same response from every audience. You can use an ad-lib to make it funny. Ad-libs in show business are not all off-the-cuff comments that you just happened to think of on the spot. They are prepared lines for low spots in the act. I have a few of these "saver" lines in the comedy section of this book. Use them sparingly, but use them.

Vary your script lines so that there are high points and low points in the laughs. Every line does not have to be a joke. Use the material so that it builds to the punch line. Use some surprise or suspense if you can get it; then suddenly relax the tension with some straight lines before going on to the next big laugh line.

Once you have decided on a routine, rehearse the act over and over again until you can remember every line and feel very much at ease using the material. The more you work, the easier it will become. Save the song or the strongest laughs for the end of the act, and build up to your finish, when you can take a long bow.

Showmanship

No matter what you do in your act, the end result should be the same—entertainment. As a performer, it is your job to sell the entertainment. Some people can entertain with magic tricks, others with jokes and songs, and you, with ventriloquism. You have an act, the gags seem to be okay, the music is right, the technique is there. But is it entertaining? How will you find out? The audience will tell you.

At no time must you allow your techniques to distract from the enjoyment of the audience. Never bore them with long-winded dialogues or too much of the same thing. For example, once you have done the telephone voice and the audience gets the message and sees how clever you are, do not drag it out with a long dialogue. Go on to the next thing. Smile, be pleasant, be human, and, of course, make your character warm and personable.

When you have done something that rates applause, stop and look at the audience for a second. Think to yourself, "Wasn't that great?" The audience will applaud. A short nod will accept the applause gracefully, so that you can go on. At the end of the act, take your bow. Don't wait for the applause; just bow. This is the signal for the audience to react.

Walk on and off the stage as though you belong there. Walk with a lively gait rather than shuffling on and off. Your hair is combed, your shoes are shined, and the figure is clean, with its clothing as neat as your own. If you look confident, the audience will have more respect for your act. Be humble and accept all compliments and applause with grace. Remember to be articulate and always use proper grammar. You must blend every theater art into your appearance.

Comedy, laughter, color, personal warmth, proper lighting, music, stage presence and appearance, timing and authority, combine to please your audience. That is showmanship.

Stagecraft

When you go before an audience, your act must be in polished form. You know the script is good, your technique flawless, the routine right. You and your partner are dressed properly, and now you are ready to walk out onto the stage. You have been introduced and you're off. But you are not alone. The helpers behind the scenes will make your act bigger and better.

Music: Your arrival on stage is accompanied by bright opening music. You should select something that gives the audience a feeling of pleasant anticipation. Use the same music all the time and it will become your theme. Have the music written in a simple, easy-to-follow orchestration for those times when you use an orchestra. A good piano melody lead sheet should be prepared for smaller dates. Do the same for any song material you need. Your opening and closing music should also have cues on the top sheet.

When you rehearse with your musicians, make sure they know all the cues, when to play each piece, and whether you need extra drum shots or chords to punctuate your difficult tricks. Make sure you are amiable and appreciative with the musicians rather than demanding that they follow your music. A good relationship with your fellow artists will insure their cooperation and they'll help make your act look even better. If no musicians are available, have a cassette tape made and amplify it.

Audio: In order for your act to be enjoyed, it must be heard. Everyone in the house must hear every word and every whisper. Your own clear diction and voice projection are fine for a small room, but when you work for many people in a nightclub, a school auditorium, or a small theater, you will need technical help. In my car I always carry an emergency portable audio system that operates on battery power for those times when the chairman of the entertainment committee forgets about microphones or supplies a lectern mike that I can't use. Your audio system is composed of your own voice, a microphone, cables to an amplifier along with a power cord to a wall socket, a good music source (tape recorder or record player), and one or more speakers. Extension cords help in large rooms.

The microphone should be one that will stand by itself or the type that fits around your neck. I prefer a small clip-on button type, and I carry adapters for various jacks so I can use the mike in any system that is available. The small mike does not distract the audience. For increased realism, have a small "dead" mike on the figure as well. When using a stand-up microphone, lower it to pick up your voice about a foot away from your mouth. You should not have to shout to be heard. And you should not have to swallow the microphone either. For an inexpensive, battery-operated sound system, you might consider the Amplivox S-310 system manufactured by the Perma-Power division of the Chamberlain Manufacturing Company in Chicago, Illinois. Your local electronics supply company can probably tell you more about these systems.

For music, a tape player is most suitable. Use C30 or C60 tapes that will carry enough music for your whole act. These can be marked so that anyone offstage can play them for you through the sound system. There are various kinds of tapes, so make sure that you have the proper player for your own cassettes or reel-to-reel tape. Eight-track players are not compatible with standard cassette players and vice versa. Carry an extra cassette in case of emergency.

Lighting: Ventriloquial figures should be seen as well as heard.

Poor lighting, like poor acoustics, will depress your audience. When you get to the theater or room where you are playing, have the electrician or technician show you the available lighting. You are best seen in white light covering the area in which you will be working. If you move about on the stage, every area you will be in must be lighted. Too much backlighting will give you the appearance of being in the dark. Too much face lighting will wash out your facial expressions. You will look good in a nice round white spot that does not glare or blind you. The lights should not be too hot or you will perspire. Have someone go out into the audience before the show begins to look at the lighting while you are onstage. If you decide to use a colored gel, a 50 percent pink shade will cut the glare of the spotlight. If you are a professional performer, you must look like one. As long as the area is lighted, and there are no shadows to distract the audience, you will be seen to good advantage.

13

SELLING THE ACT

So now you have your act; you have rehearsed it well; and you have tested it on friends and relatives and anyone else who will watch it. You feel that you are ready for the big time, working in public. How do you go about it?

Bookings

In the beginning you will have to offer your services at no charge to local groups. You can contact schools, churches, and hospitals in your area, work for charity organizations, and help entertain senior citizens. You can call or write to nursing homes, the welfare department of the American Legion, Veterans of Foreign Wars, and disabled veterans organizations. The PTAs and the Red Cross always want entertainment. Local service clubs will be happy to see your act. Try clubs such as the Elks, Moose, Odd Fellows, and so on. Your phone book will help you find them. Visit local nightclubs and speak to the owners. Many have amateur nights or talent nights for young performers.

Have a business card printed and offer it to musicians, caterers, and other people you meet in your search for a showcase. You will find that the word gets around and you'll be asked to do other "free" or "benefit" performances. When playing these dates, bring a friend who can take black-and-white photos of you in action. Let him photograph you and the audience watching you. These photos will be valuable later on.

You will also find that if you do a good show, people will come up to you and ask for your business card. They will ask if you are available for their private parties or club functions. Accept these dates for a fee. Start with a reasonable price. Check with other local entertainers to see what the going rate is. You may have to ask for less money at first, but try not to undercut the professional price by much. Remember that you yourself will soon be a professional and you do not want to set too low a value on your services.

Remember to save all programs, photos, and any publicity you get from benefit shows. If you have a few good photos and some printed reviews or mentions, you can paste them up and have copies made for a flyer you can then send out. You can take small ads in the classified section of your local paper, advertising the fact that you are available for parties and such. The best time to advertise is a few weeks before major holidays when people have parties, such as Easter, Halloween, or Christmas. Keep working, even if you don't make a great deal of money.

Your phone book will have the name and number of some theatrical booking agencies. A personal visit to the booker is best. Bring along all your photos and whatever publicity you have acquired. Show business is a business. You are the product that must be sold. You can be sold door to door, by yourself, or through an agent or distributor (the booker). Your sales will be made by advertising and by direct mail.

Have a professional photo taken by a good photographer. The picture should show you and your figure in action. You must be doing something interesting rather than just posing. Have your figure talking, or hold a prop in your hand. Both of you should look lively. When you have selected the proper picture, have it made into an eight-by-ten glossy print. Black and white is better than color for reproduction. Send the negative or a clean print to a good photo service that can reproduce it for you in quantity. These companies can usually produce twenty-five or more copies. Order only enough to cover your immediate needs. You can always reprint them, and later on you may decide to use a different or better photo. Check some of the trade newspapers, such as *Variety,* for the names of nearby photo services.

Once you have been booked through a booking agent, he will probably come to see you perform. If you are good, of course, he will try to sell you again. The booker will get a percentage of your fee, or you can both establish a price for your performance. Call on several bookers. You do not need an agent immediately. Once you have started getting paying jobs, you will probably want to join a trade union. The American Guild of Variety Artists (AGVA) covers most variety acts. The American Federation of Television and Radio Artists (AFTRA) covers television performers, and the Screen Actor's Guild (SAG) protects those who work on filmed commercials or other films. The three groups have reciprocal working agreements so that you can appear in various media. The unions establish minimum salaries and benefits and handle contractual agreements or disputes. You may also consider joining the Society of American Ventriloquists (write to Mark Wade, 414 Oak Street, Baltimore, Ohio 43105).

Publicity

Keeping your name or photo in the public eye is very important for the performer. Once you have a booking that may have some kind of news value, you can start getting into print. Send out a press release to the local papers in the area in which you are playing. The first paragraph of the press release must cover the major details. The five *w*'s represent the facts you need to tell in your first few sentences: who, what, when, where, why. Who is performing? What will happen? When will it take place? Where is it happening? Why is it important? (See Figure 34).

```
VENTRILOQUIST TO WORK AT CHARITY BALL


Talented ventriloquist John Jones will help raise funds
          1              1                       2
on December 15, at 7 PM at the Civic Auditorium for
        3                            4
the victims of this year's flood in Middletown.
        5
```

Fig. 34

110

Always type your information and story neatly, double-spaced, on a white sheet of standard typing paper. Put a headline at the top to tell the editor what you are announcing. The first line tells the basic story. In the following paragraph, offer more details about the wonderful thing you are doing by helping the victims of the flood, the name of the organization involved, the names of the leaders of the group sponsoring the show, and some idea of what a person can expect if he attends. The paragraphs should be arranged to present information in descending order of importance—with the most important first—since editors generally cut material from the bottom up when space is short. On the bottom line of your press release, print your name, address, and telephone number:

"For more information contact John Jones at . . ."

You can include a photo with your release. A four-by-five black-and-white glossy will do nicely. Wait a few days and then phone the editor and ask him if he got your note and if there is room to print it. If it does get into print, buy a few clean copies of the paper and clip the article for future use so you can build a publicity portfolio.

Let's assume that the story did run in the paper. If the event at which you performed was a big success, write an immediate follow-up story and send it to the paper. Many times the paper will run it as a feature. Let's assume you did a show at a hospital and have a few good photos. Your headline and first sentence might read:

LAUGHTER WORKS BETTER THAN MEDICINE

The laughs did better than the pills as ventriloquist John Jones and Willy served up large doses of healthy fun at (name of hospital).

Describe the show in detail and submit this and a good photo of you, the figure, and some smiling patients. If you can visit the newspaper office, deliver your material to the editor personally. The staff may rewrite your story their own way, but you have the publicity you need. Whenever you can, get a photographer to cover your story. Always try to be courteous and never pushy with the people at the paper. If you have any newsworthy ideas, work them up carefully and then offer them. Newspapers need feature material all the time. You might also send quips and jokes to some of the columnists. They will publish them with your name and you will earn a reputation as a funny guy or gal.

While on tour promoting one of my books on magic, I visited newspaper offices around the country. I carried a portable Sawing Illusion in a small suitcase. In every city in which I appeared, I visited the paper (by appointment), and with every interview I had a photographer ready to capture the reporter being sawed in half on his desk. The same stunt was done on television shows, but the newspaper articles were reprinted and used for my publicity brochure long after the television coverage was forgotten.

The late Paul Stadelman was a master at getting publicity for Windy Higgins. Paul ran a campaign to get his figure on the ballot for governor of Kentucky in 1939. Windy actually got 144 votes on a write-in ballot. When Paul gave blood for a Red Cross drive, Windy Higgins was in the photo looking on, and it made the papers. Windy sold war bonds, visited army camps, and was photographed everywhere he went. Some of Paul's publicity is reproduced here to give you an idea of how to put together a good publicity flyer (Figures 35, 36, 37).

Ventriloquist Tommy Windsor took his figure to the barbershop for a haircut. The photo made the local papers. In Dublin, Ireland, Eugene Lambert applied for a driver's license in the name of Finnegan, his vent partner. When it was discovered, Mr. Lambert was fined, but the publicity made up for his expense. In 1937 singer Sally Osman sued her husband, Herbert Dexter, for divorce. Dexter's figure, Charley, was named as correspondent. She claimed that "Charley kept hitting her in the derrière," and that Dexter paid more attention to his figure than to her. The divorce was granted. It still isn't known whether this was a publicity stunt.

When Cowboy Eddie and two other vent figures were stolen from the trunk of his car, Howard Olson, then using the name of Chester LeRoy, notified the papers that they had been kidnapped. The thief was apprehended and charged with felony theft. Olson got coverage in the Houston press (Figure 38).

Audience Gets in the Act ... Ventriloquist Shows How

CHICAGO — ⒫ — Paul Stadelman has a new act. He calls something he calls "do-it-yourself ventriloquism."

He offers to teach any member of his audience the ancient art of voice-throwing in one easy lesson.

"I'll probably put myself out of business," he said.

But he believes getting the audience into the act is the first really new twist to ventriloquism since cavemen began bouncing echoes off the cavern walls.

Stadelman is an ingenious gent who once ran his dummy for governor of Kentucky. Now he has come up with a simplified voice-tossing technique.

At a restaurant the other night he got two men and a woman up from the audience and introduced them to a pint-sized dummy named Junior Higgins.

Results Surprisingly Good

Stadelman taught his volunteers how to work the controls to make Junior's head and lips move. Next he had them practice speaking in a squeaky voice.

Then he handed each a script—one of those cross-fire conversations between ventriloquist and dummy.

The results were so good it surprised even the volunteer ventriloquists.

Stadelman said the secret lies principally in the script. He wrote it to eliminate most of the hard words, so that the average person could go through the recitation and keep his lip movements to a minimum.

Professionals, on the other hand, pride themselves on their ability to pronounce most of the letters of the alphabet without lip movement.

They All Remember Windy

Like a lot of ventriloquists, Stadelman lives in the shadow of his star dummy, a bombastic little blockhead named Windy Higgins. Back in 1939 Windy got 144 votes when Stadelman filed his name for governor.

A veteran of 30 years in show business, Stadelman has spent the last 18 as guardian, valet, mechanic and "voice" for Windy.

"The audience always remembers Windy," he complained. "But they can't even remember my name."

He once tried making Windy the straight man and telling the jokes himself, but the results were less than spectacular.

"You couldn't top me with a stepladder," Windy told his master.

Finally, Stadelman changed his billing to "Paulstad, vocal illusionist."

So what happens? The other night he was introduced as "Paul Haulsted, vocalist."

AT LAST! A VENTRILOQUIST WHO DARES TO BE DIFFERENT!

© 1956 PAUL STADELMAN

Fig. 35 Sample publicity sheets reprinted from "Ventriloquism of Today" by permission.

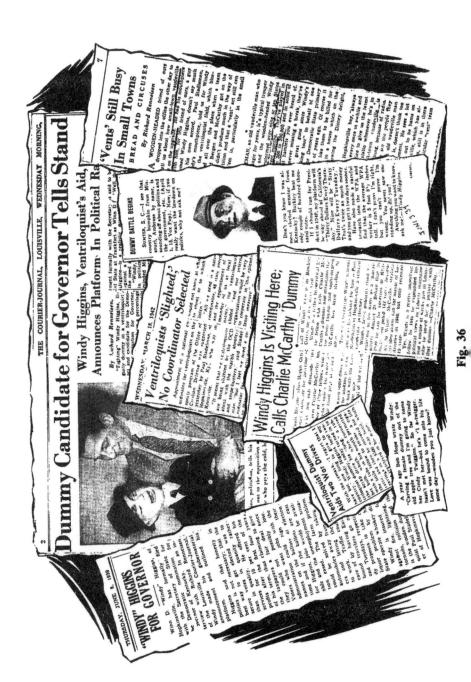

Fig. 36

His Bridey Past Is Aged In the Wood

WINDY HIGGINS, a ventriloquist's dummy with political ambitions, now imagines he has a Bridey Murphy background.

"If this doesn't elect me governor of some state that needs a governor, nothing ever will," says Windy through the unmoving lips of Chicagoan Paul Stadelman.

"Windy once was a dummy candidate for governor of Kentucky," says Stadelman whose hypnotic ability almost brought about Higgins' mental retrogression.

Be that as it may, Windy was rejected in his gubernatorial—and publicity—bid. This time, Paul says:

"Any resemblance to the Bridey Murphy case is not coincidental, but deliberate."

So away we go!

Windy, of course, regressed to his gubernatorial campaign. He spouted:

"I realize that every candidate must have a platform of some kind, so I have decided to build mine of wood. In that way I can use a lot of my relatives and in return when I am elected, they can use me."

Stadelman interspersed at this point and said:

"Relax and listen to me. Let's go back about 10 years. What are you doing?"

"I am inr a night club dressing room and you are complaining to the manager because of billing. Just then a girl dancer came in.

"I listen to you 'talk to her. Boy, you are a WOW!"

"What do you mean by WOW?" Paul asked.

"A worn out wolf," answered Windy.

"Let's not get personal," said Paul. "Can you remember when you were a tree in the forest?"

"Sure I can remember," laughed Windy.

"I can remember the exact time it happened, when the man chopped down the tree and also I remember all the dogs I used to hate. Everything is very clear."

The ventriloquist must have felt like amateur hypnotist Morey Bernstein, when Bridey Murphy made her revelation. He exclaimed:

"This is wonderful, tell me all about it!"

"Don't be silly," said Windy. "You know trees can't talk."

Winn D. "Windy" HIGGINS

WINDY was once a dummy candidate for governor of Kentucky.

DRAWING BY BILL LORING

CHICAGO AMERICAN
Sun., July 29, 195—15

Fig. 37

Fig. 38 Part of a Chester LeRoy brochure.

Gather all the notices, reviews, and publicity along with a few good photos and make up a brochure. Use an 8½-by-11 sheet that can be folded to fit in a number 10 envelope. Make sure that your printer reproduces all the photos correctly. Don't try to do this yourself with a quick printing service unless they make velox copies of your photos. Add some brief, clear copy to tell your reader about yourself and to say that your act is available for bookings. Have the type set, rather than using a typewriter. If you have to do your own layout, use clear rub-on (press type) lettering for your headlines. Do not print your address on the brochure but leave space for it to be rubber-stamped later. The space will allow the bookers to use their own names when selling the act. Do not print too many brochures at first. You may want to reprint it later with updated press clippings or photos.

Mail your brochures to prospective clients. Go back to the service clubs, PTAs, and local nightclubs, but this time ask for your professional fee.

14

COMEDY MATERIAL

The "stock" material that follows can be used to fill any blank spaces in your routine or to provide you with ideas for switching. Ad-libs can be used for those special times when you need a quick line. The double gags will supplement some of the scripts. Sprinkle your act with some of these tested laugh lines.

Opening Lines

Will the lady with the lucky number come up and take me.

I just saw the funniest comedian in the world at work. I was rehearsing in front of my mirror.

On behalf of the management—and believe me, I'd like to be half of the management.

This is a nice place. I like the way it's laid out. I don't know how long it's been dead, but I like the way it's laid out.

After such a wonderful introduction I can hardly wait to hear what I'm going to say.

As I stand here tonight, in my heart there is a burning sensation.
I guess I ate too fast.

Thanks for the applause. You folks really know talent, don't you?

It's a pleasure to be here. I enjoy looking into those nice faces. And some of your faces *need* looking into.

Ad-Libs

Memorize a few of these and drop them into your routine when you think you need them. For example, if a line does not get a laugh when it should, use a "saver." Allow the figure to use the gag.

After applause (line spoken by figure):
Not too loud, you'll wake up my ventriloquist.
Thank you very large.
I *knew* we were working too cheap.
Can you imagine what we could do if *he* had talent?

When you fluff or miss a line:
Don't laugh folks; that's the way it was written.
That's what you get doing old jokes. His *tongue* fell asleep.
Why don't you leave *me* alone and open *your* mouth?

Closing line:
On your way home, folks, drive very carefully. You've been so nice, we'd hate to lose you.

Savers:
This is an English-speaking audience, isn't it?
Is this an audience or a jury?
No silent laughing out there. If you smile, make noise.
Four score and seven years ago, our material was new.
I know you're out there. I hear you breathing.
There's nothing like new material. I wish I had some.
Turn up the power, Sam; they can't hear us out there.

Lines for Hecklers

The first rule when dealing with a heckler is to realize that he is merely trying to get attention. The best way to deflate his ego is

119

to ignore him altogether. This will not work, of course, if you are dealing with a drunk whose senses are so dull that he doesn't understand. Try to be polite, but when the wise guy becomes annoying, shoot him down with your prepared lines. Note that the use of the word *dummy* here is meant to be derogatory. Your figure should use these single lines.

> One dummy at a time, please.
> Say, who's working your head?
> I'm a dummy; what's your excuse?
> I don't usually forget a face, but in your case I'll make an exception.
> How come you're out so late? No school tomorrow?

Songs and Poems

These lines can be sung Calypso style with a vamp background or used as short poems.

> My father's name is Ferdinand;
> My mother's name is Liza.
> So naturally when I was born
> They called me Fertilizer.

> Gunga Din . . . Gunga Din . . .
> If the door is locked . . .
> How are you Gunga Din?

> As I was walking up the stairs
> I met a man who wasn't there.
> He wasn't there again today;
> I really wish he'd stay away.

> Some folks like to be in the ballet
> And dance upon their toes.
> I'd rather be an elephant
> And squirt water through my nose.

> Under the spreading Chestnut tree
> The musician played his fiddle.

A coconut fell from the top of the tree
And parted his hair in the middle.

Parodies

Home, home on the range,
Where the deer and the antelope play;
When it's thirty below
And those giant winds blow
I like to sit home on the range.

My Bonnie lies over the gas tank
The height of its contents to see.
I lighted a match to assist her.
Oh, bring back my Bonnie to me. *(Audience joins chorus.)*

The Wendy Song . . . Wendy moon comes over the mountains . . .

Double Gags

I passed your house yesterday
Thanks.

Don't these musicians ever work?
Sure. What do you think they're doing now?
Playing!

When I was a little boy . . .
Boy, what a memory!

The ship went into the sea.
Into the sea?
Yes, into the sea.
Who saw it?
I saw it.
Saw the sea?
No, the ship.

The ship saw the sea?
No. I saw the ship in the sea.
See-saw, margery daw . . . *(recite poem)*.

Be quiet.
You don't want me to be quiet. I earn you a good living.

Can you count to ten? I'll bet you can't.
I sure can. Listen. One . . . two . . . three . . . four . . .
    six . . .
What happened to five?
Don't rush; I'm coming to it.

We'll rent a car. A U-Drive.
I should drive?
No. I said U-Drive.
Why do I have to drive?
You don't drive it. *I* drive it.
Drive what?
The U-Drive.
Why should I drive, if you wanna drive?
You drive me crazy.
With you it's a short trip.

My father slipped on the ice.
What did he say?
Shall I leave out the cuss words?
Yes.
He didn't say anything.

What's your name?
Harry.
Harry?
I said it first.
You're very ignorant.
That's nothing. So am I.

Why don't you turn your back to the audience?
Why should I do that?
So they won't see your lips moving.

When are you going to leave?
When I'm good and ready.
Fine. Now I'll sing my song.
Now I'm ready.

(Bark)
What's that for?
I'm a dog.
You're not a dog.
I am so. I'm a Schnauzer.
It's all in your mind. Say it to yourself, "I am not a dog."
I am not a dog.
See? It works. Do you feel better?
I feel great; feel my nose.

I just made twenty dollars.
Honestly?
I wish you wouldn't bring that up.

Say, who gave me the TV set on Christmas?
Santa Claus, of course.
Well he was here this morning and said the next payment is
    due.

Look at that lady's wig.
That's not a wig; her hair is set.
What time does it go off?

Air pollution is awful. I don't water my flowers.
What do you do with them?
Dust 'em.

So, you're here already?
I came early today.
I'm glad to see you're early of late. You used to be behind
    before.
Now I'm first, at last.

Can you tell me what has seven legs, thirty arms, two heads,
    and speaks Italian?

I don't know; what is it?
I don't know either. I only make up the questions, not the
answers.

You're a prevaricator.
Don't you call me a liar.
Who called you a liar?
You called me a liar.
You're a liar. I never called you a liar!

I'm coming to your party Saturday night.
Great. Ring the doorbell with your elbow.
Elbow? Why can't I use my finger?
If you're coming empty-handed, you can stay home.

Can you lend me ten dollars?
I don't hear well in this ear.
(Talking into other ear) Can you lend me twenty dollars?
Better go back to the ten-dollar ear.

Years ago people used to think the world was square.
And now?
Now, everybody knows it isn't square. It's crooked.

How old do you think I am?
You don't look it.

I just found a great cure for a cold. You get into a tub filled
with gasoline and light two matches.
What's the trick?
Lighting the second match!

I owe a great deal to that lady.
Your aunt?
No, my landlady.

15
SHORT SCRIPTS

Following are a group of short scripts for you to use until you develop your own routine. Enjoy them!

The Baby-Sitter

(Enter with figure already speaking.)

F: I won't do it; I won't do it!

V: What's the matter with baby-sitting?

F: I can find nicer jobs. I don't have to change diapers for a living.

V: But it's a pleasant way to spend an evening with a charming child.

F: That whistle of a kid with his screeching all night like an owl—

V: Like an owl? Who?

F: That's what he said, too.

V: He? Who?

F: He's even got you saying it.

V: Saying what?

F: Not what! Who!

V: Who are you talking about?

F: You can say *that* again.

V: You're trying to confuse me. Now cut it out. How do you know a thing about sitting if you never tried it?

F: What makes you think I never tried it? I once sat on eight babies at one time.

V: Baby-sitters don't really *sit* on babies.

F: Oh, don't we?

V: You mean you really *sat* on a baby?

F: Only way to shut him up. This was a mean kid. His folks should've left the kid and taken the stork.

V: Children are the light of our lives. They bring the spark of sunshine into a dark and gloomy room.

F: The electric company can do the same thing a whole lot cheaper.

V: Why do you complain so much?

F: Guys who change diapers . . . turn out to be gripers.

V: There you go again. This is an easy job. The kid is three years old.

F: That's 4,380 diapers.

V: He doesn't need diapers anymore. Just give him some milk and he's okay. He'll go right to sleep.

F: Milk! That's the worst thing for kids.

V: Milk is great.

F: Milk turns to cheese, cheese turns to butter, butter becomes fat—

V: Wait a minute—

F: Fat turns to sugar, sugar to syrup, and before you know it, the kid wakes up sticky.

V: Make up your mind. Will you do it?

F: Whose kid is it?

V: It's my nephew.

F: Then I won't have to worry about the milk.

V: Why not?

F: The kid's *stuck already!*

(Exit)

Baseball

(Figure is singing as you enter.)

F: Take me out to the ballgame.
Take me out to the . . .

V: Are you going into the singing business?

F: No, I just made the Little League.

126

V: That's wonderful. What do you play?

F: Baseball.

V: No, I mean in what position do you play?

F: Sort of leaning, like this. *(Bends over)*

V: Are you a pitcher?

F: No, I'm a small glass of water. What are you talking about?

V: What's your job on the team?

F: They throw the thing; I hit it.

V: The ball?

F: That's right.

V: Why didn't you say so?

F: I can't say "ball" without moving your lips.

V: What do you do out on the field?

F: I'm a rest-up.

V: You mean shortstop.

F: No. Rest-up. I run for a while and then I have to—

V: Rest up. I don't think you know anything about baseball.

F: My grandfather was with the Yankees.

V: As a bat boy.

F: As a bat.

V: A bat is a hunk of wood.

F: That's Grandpa. He really was a catcher. He sat there with his hand all swollen up. . . .

V: He was wearing a mitt.

F: Mitt what?

V: A glove.

F: He had no glove, that's why his hand—

V: Was swollen? He had a glove made of cowhide.

F: Of what?

V: Hide . . . from the cow.

F: I don't see a cow around here.

V: There is no cow around here.

F: Then why should I hide?

V: I mean the glove.

F: The glove should hide? Are you some kind of nut?

V: Never mind. Let's talk about the game. You're at the bat and you hit a high fly—

F: What kind of fly?

V: A pop fly.

F: I wouldn't hit a mother fly. Why a father?

V: You hit a high ball. The first baseman runs in to catch it. He drops the ball. Where do you go?

F: To make a telephone call. I never hit a ball like this before. I have to tell my mother.

V: No. You run to first. Now the batter comes up and hits a fast ball. They can't get it. You run to second, then you run to third. The batter is right behind you. Now where do you go?

F: Home.

V: Right! You go home to score.

F: No, I go home to hide. That guy is still chasing me.

V: He's only chasing you to the plate.

F: The devil he is. I owe him ten dollars.

V: Now you're at the plate.

F: And we eat. Great. I'm hungry.

V: It's too late. You're out.

F: That's a great idea.

V: What is?

F: Going out! I had enough of this game. Too rough. You do it.

V: Do what?

F *(singing): Take me out to the ball game. . . .*
(Exit)

Nursery Rhymes

(Figure is speaking as you enter.)

F: I don't think it's a good idea. Kids don't want to hear those terrible things.

V: What's so horrible about nursery rhymes?

F: They are sad and unhappy.

V: What is so sad? What about the old lady who lived in a shoe?

F: See? That's sad. She had so many children she didn't know what to do. So she went around hitting kids. Nice kids too. I knew 'em.

128

V: That's not a very good example.

F: Give me a better one.

V: Okay. Let's take Humpty Dumpty.

F: Another sad story. I feel sorry for Humpty.

V: What do you mean?

F: He was a good egg.

V: He was sitting on a wall.

F: And the poor guy goes to pieces. And who helps him? No one!

V: All the king's horses and all the king's men.

F: Didn't do a thing for him. Left the poor guy bleeding his yolk out!

V: Let's pick another one. How about Miss Muffet?

F: You mean old "scairdy cat" Muffet?

V: She sat on her tuffet.

F: What's a tuffet? And be careful with your answer; we may be on TV.

V: It's a . . . a . . . I don't know what a tuffet is. Anyway, she was eating her curds and whey.

F: What are curds and whey?

V: Well, curds—that's the part of the milk that didn't coagulate.

F: What does that mean?

V: It's what's left over after the whey is taken out.

F: Now I know what it is. It's what it sounds like.

V: Curds and whey.

F: Slop. Yugh. What a horrible thing for kids.

V: Okay. How about this one? Rub-a-dub-dub, three men in a tub.

F: That's a rotten way to take a bath.

V: They weren't *taking* a bath.

F: That's not sanitary—three men in one tub.

V: And who do you think they be?

F: I'm afraid to guess.

V: The butcher, the baker . . .

F: And the candlestick maker. Three dirty old men.

V: They're not dirty old men.

F: Then why are they taking a bath?

V: They're sailing.

F: In a tub?

V: It's just a story for children. It's not true.

F: That's not right, lying to little children. Tell us one that is true.

V: Okay. Once I went up the hill with a girl named Jill to fetch a pail of water. But when we came down . . .

F: You broke your crown?

V: No. When we came down we took the water, added some syrup, and had some sodas.

F: Boy. That's what I call a true story. Let's go home and do the same.

(Exit)

Sailing

F: I hope you won't miss me when I'm gone.

V: Where are you going?

F: I'm going to Europe—on a sailboat.

V: Europe?

F: All the way to Europe by rail.

V: Just a minute; you said by sailboat. By rail means by train.

F: When I'm on this boat I lean over the rail.

V: What's the name of this ship?

F: It's called the S.S.

V: The S.S. what?

F: Nothing. Just the S.S.

V: They paint the name on the side of the ship. What did it say on the side?

F: S.S. There was no room for anything else; it was a little ship.

V: It should have a name. What do they call it?

F: Okay, we'll call it Club Sandwich.

V: Why call it that?

F: It has three decks.

V: If it has three decks it's a large ship.

F: Two of them were decks of cards.

V: How's the food?

F: Yuch.

V: Was I wrong to bring it up?

F: On this ship almost everybody brings it up.

V: You mean the ship isn't smooth sailing?

F: You heard of rock and roll? This ship invented it.

V: Sounds rough.

F: Last week the wind was blowing; the waves were coming up onto the deck; it was rocking, rolling, tossing . . .

V: How far out were you?

F: We hadn't left the dock. We were tossing two miles an hour.

V: That's not miles, that's knots.

F: You're right. You gotta be knots to go on this ship.

V: Then why go on the trip?

F: It's the cheapest way to get to Europe.

V: What fun is it, if you get there sick?

F: I *have* to get sick.

V: Why is that?

F: So I can look like my (passport)* photo.

V *(take photo out of figure's pocket):* Why, this looks a good deal like you.

F: That's a Christmas tree.

V: Oh, the green had me fooled.

F: That's how I'll look after the trip. Well, I gotta fly.

V: You mean you want to go by plane now?

F: No, I wanna fly outta here. I have to get insurance.

V: In case you drown?

F: I know I'll float. I take out only *fire* insurance. So long.

(Exit)

Moving Day

V: Why are you in such a big hurry to get home?

F: This is a big day. We're moving today.

F: That's a coincidence. I'm moving also.

F: Just your lips. Where are you moving to?

V: A little place on Vayesmere Boulevard. It's nice. It has a sunken living room and a—

F: Hold it! A sunken living room. How did it sink?

---

*Omit this word if you cannot pronounce it.

V: That's the way they built it.

F: And after the rain, does it go down altogether?

V: It doesn't really sink. It goes down slightly.

F: We'll have to get my Uncle Harry.

V: What for?

F: He's a skin diver. He can go under when the living room sinks.

V: It doesn't really sink. That's just an expression. Now we also have a raised terrace.

F: You'll need it. It's a good place to jump up onto when the living room sinks.

V: The living room doesn't sink. Now it overlooks the park.

F: My place also overlooks.

V: Overlooks what?

F: Hot water, steam heat, a bathroom.

V: No bathroom? That's impossible.

F: It's *un-canny*. But I have a sunken—

V: A sunken what?

F: I don't know. We haven't dragged it up yet.

V: You're kidding. The only thing I don't care for is the bus on my block going back and forth, back and forth.

F: You can stop that back and forth business.

V: How?

F: Move to a one-way street.

V: My bedroom is great. It's out of this world.

F: How do you get to bed, by rocket ship?

V: You know what I mean. I only wish the room was larger.

F: We made our place a lot larger.

V: How did you do it?

F: We scraped off the wallpaper.

V: Well, I'd better be going. I have to fill up those packing cylinders.

F: I had one once that got caught in my eye.

V: What got caught in your eye?

F: A small piece of cylinder, probably blew out of the fire.

V: That's a cinder. I'm talking about a cylinder.

F: Oh, a slinder . . . tall and thin.

V: That's slender. I mean a cylinder.

F: A cylinder? What's a cylinder?

V: You don't know what a cylinder is?

F: Is it round?

V: Does your sister wear earrings?

F: Sure.

V: What shape are they?

F: Square on the weekdays.

V: And on Sundays?

F: Round.

V: You know what round is, and you know what square is, and if you think a little you can figure out the shape of a cylinder.

F: I got it.

V: Good.

F: Square on weekdays, round on Sundays.

V: Let's move.

(Exit)

Spanish Astronaut

V: Come on, it's time for your Spanish lesson.

F: Who needs Spanish? I wanna be an astronaut.

V: That's silly; you can't be an astronaut. You're too young.
Now repeat after me—*uno, dos, tres* . . .

F: *Tres, dos, uno.*

V: What're you doing?

F: A Spanish countdown, *tres, dos, uno,* cha, cha, cha. cha.

V: That's ridiculous.

F: Blast off. *(Rotate head completely around on socket.)*

V: You don't know anything about space or astronomy.

F: I know *all about* astronomy.

V: Like what?

F: Like it's great with mustard and rye bread and pickles.

133

V: That's pastrami. What do you know about stars?

F: They get a lot of money on TV.

V: Let's get to the Spanish. How do you say bull-fighter?

F: Cuspidore *(pronounce "cusp-i-dore")*.

V: Not cuspidore. It's *toreador.* Now let's get it straight.

F: Revolving door. What do I care? I'm going to the moon.

V: You'll have to learn languages to be an astronaut.

F: Do they speak Spanish on the moon?

V: There's no one up there.

F: What about the man in the moon? He's up there.

V: There are just craters up there.

F: That's him. Judge Crater.

V: The moon is covered with dust.

F: Sounds like your living room. I'll need a helmet.

V: You're not going to the moon, see?

F: *Si, si, si;* that's Spanish.

V: *Vamos a comer!*

F: I agree.

V: I said, "Let's eat."

F: That's where I'm going. Out to launch.

(Exit)

Safety Script: Cross at the Green

Many ventriloquists work for small children in school auditoriums and present programs with many different messages. Choose your message and work it into your routine. Here is one example.

V: Well, here we are at *(name of place).*

F: I'd rather be in Tulsa.

V: What's in Tulsa?

F: My father is in Tulsa.

V: I see. What's his name?

F: Same as mine?

V: What's your name?

F: Same as my father's name, only younger.

V: Where do you live?

F: With my father and mother.

V: Do they live in Tulsa?

F: No, they live with me.

V: Where do you all live?

F: Together!

V: This is not getting us anywhere.

F: Where are you going?

V: I'm not going anywhere.

F: Well, be careful getting there; it's dangerous.

V: Getting where is dangerous?

F: Just crossing the street is dangerous.

V: Not if you know the rules.

F: What rules?

V: You must cross at the green, and not in between.

F: That's cute; say it again.

V: Cross at the green and not in between. Do you know what that means?

F: To run on the yellow is suicide, fellow.

V: Something like that. When the light is red, what do you do?

F: Let me see now. I could . . . I could . . . *(thinking)*

V: When the traffic light turns red, you stop. When it turns green, you can walk.

F: What do I do with my car?

V: You don't have a car.

F: Then how did I get there?

V: Don't confuse me. I'll bet the kids in the audience know the rules of crossing the street.

F: Stop, look, and listen.

V: Right. Let's test them. *(To children in the group)* What do you do when the light turns red? *(Wait for them to shout)* Stop! Very good. We wait until green and then we . . . *(point to the group)* Go!

F: They don't like me.

V: Of course they do. Why do you think they don't like you?

F: They want me to go.

V: No they don't.

F: Yes they do. Watch. Hey kids, what shall I do when the light turns green? *(They'll yell, "Go!")*

135

F: You see?

V: Have you got anything to say before we go?

F: Don't lose your head, when the light turns to red. The delay is not as long as it may seem. When it's yellow, just wait; you won't be late. Just remember to cross at the green.

(Exit)

Talking Crow

(Use a crow or any bird figure.)

V: I'd like you to meet my little friend. A strange bird. What's your name?

F: Caw *(sound like a crow)*.

V: I said, what's your name?

F: Caw. My name is Caw.

V: Oh, I'm sorry.

F: *You're* sorry? How do you think I feel?

V: I think that's a pretty good name for a bird. What kind of bird are you?

F: A chicken.

V: That's ridiculous. You're not a chicken.

F: I'm not? That's funny; I get ninety cents a dozen for my eggs.

V: Stop kidding. What kind of bird are you?

F: A seven-forty-seven.

V: That's a plane.

F: I can fly as high as he can.

V: I doubt that. How can you fly so high?

F: I drink.

V: Stop kidding. You look like a crow.

F: You don't look so good yourself, kid!

V: Where do you come from?

F: An egg.

V: I know that. I mean what city or state?

F: Anchorage, Kentucky.

V: Anchorage is in Alaska.

F *(surprised):* No kidding? When did it move?

V: What were you doing in Alaska?

F: I used to be a penguin.
V: What happened?
F: My tuxedo got lost at the cleaners.
V: You're just pulling my leg.
F: You do look a little taller.
V: You must be hungry. I'll bet you like corn.
F: If I didn't, would I be doing this act?
V: Why don't you sing a little song, and we'll leave.
F: Okay. *(Sings)* I'm only a bird in a girdled cage. . . .
V: That's *gilded.*
F: You wear what you like, and I'll wear what I like.
V: I'm sorry; go ahead.
F *(sings):* Come fly with me. . . .
V: Which way?
F: As the crow flies. Why don't you give up show business and go straight.
V: Sing your song.
F *(sings):* If you knew Susie, like I know Susie. *(Talk)* Shame on you.
V: Sing.
F: Sing?
V: Sing!
(Into song and exit)

Libraries

(Set a few books on a shelf behind you.)
V: Well, *(name of figure),* here we are at the library. How do you like it here?
F: Too quiet in here.
V: Of course it's quiet. All libraries are quiet.
F: Are they afraid to wake up the books?
V: No. It's just that people don't want to be disturbed while they read.
F: Are they all asleep?
V: They're just being quiet.
F: *(shouts loudly):* Hello, everybody!
V: What are you doing?
F: I think they're dead.

137

V: Come on now; stop kidding around. Would you like to read a book or something?

F: I just read a very sad story.

V: A sad story? What story was it?

F: My report card.

V: You're impossible. Here we are in a building alive with hundreds of stories—

F: You wanna go upstairs?

V: What's upstairs?

F: That's another story.

V: You don't know anything about books, do you?

F: Ask me anything.

V: Okay. What did you read? Did you like *Little Women?*

F: I sure do. More than reading books.

V: That's the name of a famous book. Do you know what it's about?

F: Midgets?

V: No! I'm surprised at you. Why, when I was younger I always had my nose in a book.

F: Why didn't you carry a handkerchief?

V: You're really terrible.

F: I used to belong to the Book-of-the-Day Club.

V: You mean Book-of-the-Month.

F: No, Book-of-the-Day. It's for fast readers.

V: I wonder if you even know how to read.

F: Are you kidding? I'm a first-grade reader.

V: Do you read well?

F: As well as anyone else in the first grade.

V: Do you know the alphabet?

F: Inside out—from *A* to *B.*

V: Just as I thought! You're illiterate.

F: Not only that; I can't read.

V: Okay. We'll teach you. *(Take a piece of paper out of your pocket as though showing it to the figure.)* Here are the letters.

F: See if there's a letter from my sister.

V: This is the alphabet. Now this first one is *A.*

F: I know that one. It looks like a tent with a chinning bar.

V: Yes it does. Here's a *B* and a *C*.

F: *(in a rhyme):* And a *D* and an *E* and a one, two, three.

V: There's an *F* and a *G*.

F: And an *H, I, J. (still in sing-song);* then there's a *K.*

V: *L, M, N, O.*

F: What was that?

V: I said *O.*

F *(sings):* Oh, what a beautiful morning.

V: You're not even paying attention. I suppose you'd rather sing.

F: I sure would. *(Whispers)* La, la, la.

V: I can't hear you.

F: We're in a library; I have to be quiet.

V: Okay, sing so everyone can hear you.

F: I'd like to sing a song about the alphabet. The One Eye song.

V: One Eye song?

F: One Eye-rish eyes are smiling.

V: Sing anything you like.

F: *(Closes with a song).*

(Exit)

An Interview

(Boy or girl figure)

V: Ladies and gentlemen, at this time I wish to thank you for my engagement here tonight.

F: You're engaged? Is she nice looking?

V: Please. When I say I'm engaged, I don't mean to be married.

F: What's wrong with being married?

V: Never mind. Let's do a sort of impromptu interview.

F: Impromptu? We rehearsed like crazy.

V: Now, *(name of figure),* where were you born?

F: In a hospital.

V: No, I mean in what city?

F: In *what* city?

V: Yes. In which city were you born?

139

F: Which city? First it's what city, now it's which city. Why don't you make up your mind?

V: Where did you come from?

F: Did you ever hear the story of the birds and the bees, sonny?

V: What I mean is, what is the geographical location?

F: Well it's . . . the *what? (Does a double-take)*

V: Geographical location.

F: We never had one of those.

V: The name of the town.

F: Oh that. It's Woodenfalls, Indiana.

V: Woodenfalls?

F: No, it wouldn't.

V: Have you any brothers or sisters?

F: I have three sisters.

V: Three altogether?

F: No. One at a time.

V: Who are your parents?

F: Mother and Dad.

V: I mean, what does everybody call them?

F: We can get thrown outa here for that answer.

V: Let's get on. What do you do for a living?

F: I breathe.

V: Do you work?

F: I'm a prizefighter for a tobacco company.

V: A prizefighter for a tobacco company?

F: I box cigars.

V: That's a rotten joke.

F: What are you complaining about? I'm closer to it than you are.

V: Why are your cheeks so red?

F: Cause.

V: Cause what?

F: Cause-metics.

V: Are you trying to be funny?

F: That's more than you're trying to do.

V: Suppose you recite your poem.

F: Okay. Here I go. A boy sat on the Golden Gate Bridge.

V: Go on.

F: He knew he hadn't oughta.

V: And?

F: And when he took his shoes off, his feet were in the water.

V: Who wrote that?

F: Long Fellow.

(Pause) You see, his feet were in the water.

V: Sing something!

F: Though April Showers
  May come your way
  They bring the flowers
  That bloom in May.

V: Nice!

F: Those April showers
  May seem so sweet,
  You need a rowboat
  To cross the street

V: Wait a minute

F: Those April showers
  Become a pain.
  Ever change a tire
  In the rain?

V: Sing it right! *(Sings)* So if you're looking for a bluebird . . .

F: Or hunting for a feller . . .

V: Because of April showers . . .

F *(speaks out loud):* Take an umbrella.

V: Nice going, Jolson.

F: You too, Sinatra.

(Walk off to music playing "April Showers.")

16
PHOTO GALLERY 2

Dennis Alwood and his McElroy figure. Dennis is a popular West Coast performer and figure maker. He was the technical advisor for the film Magic *and taught Anthony Hopkins how to use the figure.*

Anthony Hopkins as Corky the Ventriloquist with his acid-tongued figure Fats in the movie Magic.

Colonel Bill Boley, a real Kentucky Colonel and one of the busiest vents in the South. Bill not only performs at schools and amusement parks but finds time to teach, make vent puppets, and write. His gospel scripts are widely used.

Stanley Burns and Dr. Lichi. Stanley is an author, lecturer, and vent historian. He has translated the Chapel book from French into English and has written extensively on the subject. Stan took up ventriloquism to correct a stuttering problem and is one of New York's busiest performers.

Jerry Layne has appeared in the U.S. and in Canada where he had his own television show for many years. He is currently appearing in West Coast nightclubs and recently was featured at Knott's Berry Farm in California. Jerry also makes vent figures. His first teacher was the author.

Shari Lewis and Lambchop are known all over the world. This multi-talented ventriloquist also sings, dances, and performs magic. She has her own television shows both here and in England and has performed for Queen Elizabeth in a Command Performance. Shari has also been featured wih her nightclub act in Las Vegas.

Bob Neller and Reggie, a figure that boasts twelve mechanical movements with which he can create over 4,000 facial expressions. Neller was the first ventriloquist in the United States to appear on television. He went on the air for NBC station W2XBS in New York in June, 1939.

Jimmy Nelson and friends Danny O'Day, Farfel, and Humphrey Hisbye. This talented man is no stranger to American television audiences. He has appeared in numerous commercials and was the famous Texaco announcer for the "Milton Berle Show." His work as a performer has been acclaimed by the public and by his peers for his expert technique.

Howard Olson and Cowboy Eddy. Howard started in the business while a youngster, working with his father, The Great Chesterfield. He was known as Chester LeRoy during his nightclub and vaudeville days. Olson had his own television shows in Houston, Texas, and Milwaukee and Madison, Wisconsin (Circus 3). He has toured the country working with such stars as Danny Thomas and Red Skelton. Now retired, Olson still keeps his hand in the business by teaching and making vent figures.

Dan Ritchard is a rising vent star whose technique is in the tradition of the Great Lester. His "telephone" and "distant" voice effects are perfect illusions. Dan works in New York City doing "walk-arounds" at parties and trade shows in addition to a comedy act in which Conrad plays the trumpet.

Mark Wade, accompanied by Arthur, is the National Chairman of the Society of American Ventriloquists. He is a talented performer and a collector of vent memorabilia. He is also the editor of the New Oracle, a ventriloquist publication for the S.A.V.

Paul Winchell and friends Jerry Mahoney and Knucklehead Smith. Paul began his career with Major Bowes in 1938 and rose to become America's top TV ventriloquist in the 1950s. He has also appeared as an actor in many TV and film roles. He pursued a career in medicine and is now known as Dr. Paul Winchell.

BIBLIOGRAPHY

Andrews, Val. *A Practical Guide to Ventriloquism.* Calgary, Alberta, Canada: Micky Hades, 1977.

Craggs, Douglas. *Ventriloquism from A-Z.* London: Faber & Faber, 1969.

Davie, Kevin. *Ventriloquism.* Chicago: Magic, Inc., 1978.

Falkner, Bob. *How to Become a Ventriloquist.* DeKalb, Ill.: Kingdom Kraft, 1973.

Ganthony, Robert. *Modern Ventriloquism.* London: Will Goldston, 1919.

——— *Practical Ventriloquism.* London: Uppcott, Gill, 1893.

Houlden, Douglas. *Ventriloquism for Beginners.* London: Kaye & Ward, 1967.

Hurling, Maurice. *The Concert Ventriloquist.* London: Magic Wand, 1951.

Marshall, Frances. *The Super Show.* Chicago: Magic, Inc., 1977.

McAthy, George. *New Laff-tested Dialogs.* Calgary, Alberta, Canada: Micky Hades, 1967.

Prince, Arthur. *The Whole Art of Ventriloquism.* London: Will Goldston, 1915.

Schindler, George. *Presto! Magic for the Beginner.* New York: Reiss, 1977. (Reprinted by Dover Publications, Inc.)

——— *Ventro-folio.* Brooklyn, N.Y.: Show-Biz Services, 1970.

Stadelman, Paul. *Ventriloquism of Today.* Chicago: Paul Stadelman, 1963.

Winchell, Paul. *The Key to Ventriloquism.* Owings Mills, Maryland: Ottenheimer, 1954.